KU-740-548

*Law*Basics

DELICT

AUSTRALIA
LBC Information Services—Sydney

CANADA and USA
Carswell—Toronto

NEW ZEALAND
Brooker's—Auckland

SINGAPORE and MALAYSIA
Sweet & Maxwell Asia
Singapore and Kuala Lumpur

*Law*Basics

DELICT

SECOND EDITION

by

Gordon Cameron

Lecturer in Law at the University of Dundee

First published in 2002

This edition published in 2005 by W. Green & Son Ltd
21 Alva Street
Edinburgh EH2 4PS

Printed and bound in Great Britain by MPG Books,
Bodmin, Cornwall

No natural forests were destroyed to make this product;
Only farmed timber was used and replanted

A CIP catalogue record for this book is available from the British Library

ISBN 0 414 015851

© W. Green & Son Ltd 2005

All rights reserved. United Kingdom statutory material in this publication is
acknowledged as Crown copyright.

No part of this publication may be reproduced or transmitted in any form or by
any means, or stored in any retrieval system of any nature without prior written
permission, except for permitted fair dealing under the Copyright, Designs and
Patents Act 1988, or in accordance with the terms of a licence issued by the Copy
right Licensing Agency in respect of photocopying and/or reprographic
reproduction. Application for permission for other use of copyright material
including permission to reproduce extracts in other published works shall be made
to the publishers. Full acknowledgment of author, publisher and source must be
given.

This edition is dedicated to my brother Colin who paid good money for a copy of the first.

CONTENTS

TABLE OF CASES

1. INTRODUCTION

THE PLACE OF DELICT IN SCOTS LAW

Delict and public law
Delict is an aspect of private as opposed to public law. This means that the law of delict regulates relations between private legal persons whether individuals or corporations as opposed to relations between the individual and the state. That said, civil remedies may be sought where state agencies have acted wrongfully and this brings delict into contact with administrative law which is a branch of public law. This is a developing area of the law given fresh impetus by Human Rights legislation.

Delict and criminal law
A clear distinction may be drawn between civil law, of which delict is part, and criminal law which is another element of public law. Delict and criminal law both concern wrongdoing, but in different senses. Delict consists of a breach of a duty owed to another person or a wrongful act against another person. A crime is an offence against the criminal law. Because delict necessarily involves some form of invasion of another person's rights and is not simply a transgression of the law there can be no such thing as a victimless delict.

There are some areas of overlap, for example, an assault may be the subject both of criminal proceedings and a civil action. An offence against the criminal law, however, is not necessarily a delict and a delict is not necessarily a crime. While in a criminal trial the prosecution must prove its case *beyond reasonable doubt*, in a civil case sufficient proof may be established on *the balance of probabilities*.

Where one person suffers loss as a consequence of wrongful behaviour and liability in delict is established the wrongdoer or delinquent comes under an obligation to repair the harm. Thus the term reparation may be used instead of delict. Reparation however normally refers to monetary compensation in the form of damages and there are of course other remedies available in delict that may prove more suitable in the circumstances. In the modern law the aim of damages is to compensate the victim, not to penalise the wrongdoer. The criminal law imposes penalties and is mobilised by agents of the state who prosecute the accused in the criminal courts. The law of delict is mobilised by citizens or other legal individuals and remedies, not penalties, are pursued in the civil courts.

Objectivity and the mental element
Liability in reparation under the common law requires *culpa*, that is, fault not *mens rea*. In criminal law mental fault (*mens rea*) is required in order

to justify punishment. Because the law of delict does not punish, this need for inquiry into the state of mind of the delinquent does not arise. Nevertheless, a rough comparison may be made. In the modern criminal law the tendency is to judge *mens rea* objectively by the standard of the reasonable person rather than to look for corrupt and evil intention. In reparation the mental element concerns what the defender ought to have known or ought to have foreseen. Thus, as in the criminal law, the approach taken is objective.

When enquiring into harm caused unintentionally the question is whether a reasonable person in the position of the defender would have foreseen that their acts or omissions involved a risk of injury to the pursuer. Broadly, where there is a foreseeable risk there is a duty to take care although this statement requires qualification as will become evident in the chapter on negligence. It is not a defence to establish that the defender did not in fact foresee a risk if they ought to have foreseen it, and what ought to have been foreseen is determined by reference to what the reasonable person would have foreseen.

When considering intentional harm it appears in most cases that the specific or direct intention to harm the pursuer need not be present, but establishing *culpa* (fault) is dependent upon knowledge that the defender ought to have possessed. Intentional conduct may be culpable where an action is carried out deliberately in the knowledge that harm to the pursuer will be the likely result, irrespective of care taken. There appears to be no need to enquire into whether the defender did in fact know that harm would be the inevitable consequence; such knowledge can be imputed if it should have been evident to the reasonable person.

In the general case, just as in the criminal law, motive is irrelevant. However, there are exceptions in certain areas of delict. Liability for use of land *in aemulationem vicini* is dependent upon establishing malice. Malice is also the basis for liability in defamation, but, except where certain defences apply, malice is presumed and need not be proved. Motive is relevant in establishing conspiracy and in liability for inducing breach of contract.

Obligations

The Scotland Act 1998, s.126(4) divides Scots private law into the law of persons, the law of property, the law of obligations and the law of actions. This restates a Roman taxonomy. The same categories are found in Gaius' *Institutes* of A.D. 161. Delict is a branch of the law of obligations. An obligation is "a legal tie by which we may be necessitated or constrained to pay or perform something" (Stair, *Institute* III, 1).

The other branches of obligations are: contract; promise; unjustified enrichment; and *negotiorum gestio*. Contractual obligations and promise arise *ex voluntate*, that is, by the will of the person taking on the obligation. People volunteer for such obligations. Obligations arising from unjustified enrichment and *negotiorum gestio* arise *ex lege*: they are imposed by law in circumstances where justice requires that an action lie against the party enriched, but where there is no basis in agreement for a contractual obligation.

Broadly speaking, delictual obligations arise from wrongdoing. They may arise arise *ex lege*, for example, the law imposes on the occupiers of premises a duty to take reasonable care to ensure the safe condition of those premises (Occupiers' Liability (Scotland) Act 1960, s.2(1)). At the same time the obligation of reparation may be said to arise *ex culpa*, that is, from fault or wrongdoing. Stair described delictual obligations as *obediential* and contractual obligations as *conventional*.

Delictual conduct that has caused harm may give rise to a positive obligation to make reparation. Equally, obligations may be negative. People can be prevented from doing things such as breaching contractual terms or trespassing. The relevant legal remedy in such circumstances is *interdict* which is a discretionary remedy available in the courts. The terms of an interdict specify precisely conduct which is forbidden.

Obligations and property law
The law of obligations is also closely related to the law of property. Parties may agree to transfer ownership in a thing. The agreement is a contract. Contractual obligations are normally bilateral involving a corresponding relationship of rights and duties. While the agreement gives rise to the seller's duty to transfer ownership and the buyer's duty to pay, corresponding with the buyer's right to receive the thing and the seller's right to receive payment, these obligations are enforceable against the parties themselves, but not against the thing. The buyer has no right in the property until ownership is transferred.

Thus where ownership has not passed according to the terms of the contract the buyer may sue the seller for breach of contract or may seek *specific implement* to enforce the seller to deliver or convey, but if the thing has been sold to a third person the disappointed buyer has no right to possess the thing and must be content with damages for breach.

The obligation itself is not sufficient to confer a *real right*, such as ownership in the thing. For this to arise a transfer of property rights is required. Real rights, (a right in a thing, *ius in re*) arise as an operation of the law of property which is concerned with the relationship between persons and things. Obligations concern the relations between persons and other persons. Contract and delict give rise not to real rights but *personal rights* (*ius in personam*). Real rights may be vindicated against the whole world. If the property is yours, you can recover it from anybody who has acquired it. Personal rights can only be enforced against legal persons. Legal persons may be natural persons meaning individuals, but they may also be corporations or other recognised bodies, for example, a local authority or office holders, for example, the Lord Advocate.

There are areas of delict that are intimately related to property. As noted, the occupation of heritable property incurs a statutory duty to exercise reasonable care for the safety of persons entering on that property. Equally, harm to property may be the form of loss that is the subject of an action for damages.

Delict may be invoked to protect property rights. For example, the right to exclusive use and possession of heritable property may be enforced under the laws of trespass or encroachment. The right to comfortable enjoyment of heritable property is protected by the law of nuisance. Nuisance straddles property law and delict and there is no clear agreement on its proper location within private law. An operation conducted on land maliciously with the predominant spiteful purpose of harming a neighbour is actionable in delict *in aemulationem vicini.* Where excavations have deprived a neighbour's buildings of necessary support, actions have been raised in some cases in negligence, in others in nuisance. However, it has been argued that such cases should be resolved in the law of property and not delict.

Delict has a clear position within the structure of Scots law. But, like all other elements, it is not a totally discrete body of law, it inter-relates with other areas of the law, in some instances, very closely.

RIGHTS AND WRONGS

The structure of delict

Stair is aptly described as the architect of modern Scots law. It is primarily Stair whom we have to thank for a systematic exposition of Scots law that allows it to be presented according to a coherent structure in which obligations occupy a clear location in relation to other aspects of private law and contractual and delictual obligations are differentiated.

Stair introduced his treatment of delict as follows:

> "We come to the obligations by delinquences, which are civilly cognoscible by our custom, according to their known names and titles in our law; which, though they do rather signify the acts or actions, whereby such obligations are incurred or prosecuted, than the obligations themselves, yet they will be sufficient to hold out both. These are either general, having no particular name or designation: and such are pursued under the general name of damage and interest; which hath as many branches and specialties, as there can be valuable and reparable damages; besides those of a special name and nature, which are chiefly these, asythment, extortion, circumvention, defraud of creditors, spuilzie, intrusion, ejection, molestation, breach of arrestment, deforcement, contravention [of lawburrows], forgery…" (Stair Inst. I. 9, 5.)

In this passage Stair does two things. First, he provides a general action for damage and interest. Secondly, he lists a number of specific wrongs, that is, nominate delicts meaning delicts with names. The delicts listed are those operative in Scots law at the time which is towards the end of the seventeenth century. It has been argued strongly that Stair viewed these specific wrongs as examples that could be subsumed under the general action. Another view is that Scots law operates with a general principle of reparation for loss wrongfully caused plus a number of discrete delicts with their own rules for liability. When the true nature and structure of delict is considered there is scope for interpretation and debate. It is certainly clear, as Visser and Whitty state, that Stair presented the general action "in a way which made it compatible with the nominate delicts". It is also clear that there is a general principle of delictual liability and this serves to distinguish the underlying theoretical basis of Scots delict from its English equivalent, the law of torts.

Stair was ahead of his time in specifying the general action for damage and interest. He did, however provide space for the law to develop and it is during the eighteenth century that we see the development of the general action in the context of liability for personal injury caused through unintentional, but nevertheless culpable conduct. Specifically the earliest cases were brought by pursuers who had been injured falling down holes that had been left in a state where there was no protection for the unwary pedestrian.

Damnum injuria datum

The Lex Aquilia of around 287 B.C. provided a penal action arising from the forcible destruction of certain types of property including slaves. The praetors (Roman magistrates) came to allow an action by analogy with the Lex in respect of property destruction caused indirectly and by the time of the emperor Justinian in the sixth century A.D., Aquilian liability was stated in terms that covered all loss wrongfully caused.

Although Stair did not explicitly base the general action on Aquilian liability, it is clear that this civilian doctrine, especially as developed in Roman-Dutch law was of great influence upon him. Pleadings in the earliest general action cases drew specifically upon the Lex Aquilia. Thus the governing general principle of delictual liability in Scots law is said to be *damnum injuria datum*. This means loss (*damnum*) caused by (*datum*) a wrong (*injuria*).

Loss may be understood in terms of an infringement of a person's legal rights. We do not, in Scotland, have a modern comprehensive and exhaustive statement of legally protected interests in the way that is found, for instance in German Law (para.823 BGB). On the other hand Stair provided a list of reparable or protected interests, the infringement of which covers most if not all forms of loss reparable in delict.

According to Stair (*Institute* I, ix 4) , protected interests under the Scots law of delict are: (i) the right to life, members and health; (ii) the right to liberty; (iii) the right to fame, reputation and honour; (iv) the right to content, delight and satisfaction; and (v) the right to goods and possessions.

Thus personal injury or death is actionable in delict as is wrongful imprisonment and defamation. Damages in the form of *solatium* are recoverable for pain, suffering, inconvenience and affront. Damage to property is likewise reparable. The invasion of a person's right to exclusive possession of property is not *per se* reparable, but may be remedied by interdict.

An example of a later addition to protected interests is the right to the comfortable enjoyment of property free from serious disturbance and substantial inconvenience. This right was first recognised in Scots law well after Stair's time and is protected by the doctrine of nuisance. Again, the commission of nuisance does not of itself give rise to a right to damages, but is remediable through interdict.

Loss, to be reparable, must be caused *injuria*. Loss that is not caused *injuria* is termed *damnum absque injuria* and is not reparable. *Injuria* means unlawfully or without right. In some instances the requirements of delict are satisfied because the act itself is unlawful. For example, where two or more parties conspire with the predominant purpose of injuring a person's business interests or where somebody knowingly induces one person to breach a contract with another. An act of trespass by walking across a person's ground is not in itself unlawful, but it is an invasion of another person's right to exclusive possession and if conducted without legal justification is an act committed without any right to do so. On this basis trespass is actionable. Disturbing or polluting activities are not necessarily unlawful, but may be regarded as such if they interfere with a neighbour's right to comfortable enjoyment of their own property to a degree sufficiently grave to amount in law to nuisance. In this instance an act becomes unlawful only because it invades another person's legally protected interest. Negligent acts are seldom unlawful or conducted without right, but they breach a requirement to exercise care imposed by law.

Culpa

In expressing the general principle the word *injuria* has sometimes been replaced by *culpa* thus: *damnum culpa datum*, loss caused by fault. To this extent *culpa* may be seen as an exposition or development on the concept of *injuria*. It may be noted that statute may impose strict liability meaning that there is no requirement on the pursuer to prove fault, for example, in establishing liability under Pt 1 of the Consumer Protection Act 1987.

Culpa is the essential basis for liability in reparation in Scots common law. In other words no action at common law for delictual damages can succeed unless the pursuer proves *culpa* on the part of the defender. Historically there have been exceptions. Liability for harm done by animals was strict where the animal was of a kind known to cause damage or where the keeper knew of the animal's vicious propensities. Liability for certain types of harm done by certain animals remains strict, but is now placed on a statutory footing by the Animals (Scotland) Act 1987. For much of the twentieth century liability in damages for nuisance was argued to be strict, but since the House of Lords decision in *RHM Bakeries (Scotland) Ltd v Strathclyde Regional Council*, liability rests unambiguously upon *culpa*. It has been suggested that there is an exception to the general rule where property harm is consequent upon the alteration of the natural course of a stream. This view rests upon the assumption that *Caledonian Railway Co v Greenock Corporation* was determined in the absence of proof of fault. However, the unreported opinion of the Lord Ordinary (Dewar) shows that this was not the case.

The Romans contrasted *culpa*, meaning negligence with dolus meaning intended harm. In much of the Scottish case law and literature of the nineteenth and twentieth centuries the term *culpa* was indeed used as a synonym for negligence. In the modern context *culpa* is given a generic meaning which embraces both intentional and unintentional harm. This generic view of *culpa* is given detailed judicial consideration by Lord Hope in *Kennedy v Glenbelle*.

Culpa may be manifested through malice, through intentional conduct, through recklessness and through negligence. In *Kennedy v Glenbelle*, *culpa* is presented on a continuum with malice at one end, where harm to the victim is the predominant objective of the act, and negligence at the other end. In negligence there is a foreseeable risk of harm to the victim if the activity is carried out with insufficient care. Negligence consists in taking insufficient care in circumstances where the law imposes a duty to exercise care. Next to malice on the continuum is intention, meaning in this formulation, a deliberate act done in the knowledge that harm would be the likely result. Between intention and negligence is recklessness, where harm to the pursuer is very likely, but the defender carries on regardless. Negligence is differentiated from the other forms of *culpa* in this model on the basis that in negligence there is a risk of harm if sufficient care is not taken whereas in the other categories harm is certain, virtually certain or highly likely whether or not care is exercised.

This exposition on *culpa* was delivered in Scots law in the context of nuisance. This does not mean that its relevance is restricted to that doctrine though it may be anticipated that this argument could be advanced. This model derives from the United States of America where it was intended as a general treatment of fault in tort.

The modern law

While the general principle *damnum injuria datum* may be seen as the foundation of all liability in reparation it may remain helpful to see delictual liability as arising from either intentional harm on one hand or unintentional harm on the other. Unintentional harm falls under the doctrine of negligence. This is by far the most important aspect of delictual liability in the modern context. Theoretically, in Scots law there is no need to bring a claim under any particular head since loss caused wrongfully is always, in principle, reparable. In practice however we continue to present intentional forms of liability with reference to nominate heads, and some of these have rules of liability and defences that are peculiar to themselves. Defamation is perhaps the best example. A modern list of nominate delicts looks rather different from Stair's list. Assythment was abolished by the Damages (Scotland) Act 1976. Other delicts noted by Stair have become obscure such as spuilzie, and contravention of lawburrows, while nominally part of the law, is seldom if ever pursued. A definitive and exhaustive list of nominate delicts remains elusive.

2. LIABILITY FOR UNINTENTIONAL HARM

INTRODUCTION

In English law negligence is both a tort in its own right and a means whereby another tort may be committed. The situation is different in Scots law. It has been argued that Scots law does not recognise a delict of negligence. Liability in negligence in Scots law can be seen as the application of the general principle of reparation, *damnum injuria datum* in the context of unintentionally caused harm. In short, there is no delict of negligence in Scots law, but the law recognises liability for unintentional harm on the basis of the general principle.

Negligence has been characterised as a failure to take care in circumstances where care is required. However not all harm caused carelessly is reparable in law. Liability for negligence arises only in circumstances where the law imposes a legal duty to take care.

A clear example of a circumstance where the law imposes a duty of care is driving a vehicle. The act of driving always carries a risk of harm to others or their property if conducted without sufficient care. If I knock you off your bicycle, because I am looking at my passenger and not at the road then I am negligent and will be liable for any injury you suffer and for the cost of repairing or replacing your bike.

When a person embarks on an activity that is more or less certain to cause harm to others irrespective of how much care is taken this is culpable, but it is not negligent. In such circumstances *culpa* is better understood in terms of intention.

Some interests are not legally protected against unintentional acts or omissions. In the general case it is accepted that there is a duty to avoid injuring or killing persons and destroying or causing damage to their property. Other forms of harm raise specific issues and will be considered separately. Purely financial harm that is not consequential on injury to the person or property of the pursuer does not, in general give rise to liability for negligence, but there are exceptions providing certain requirements are met. Unintentional injury to mental health is reparable, but the courts have developed rules peculiar to this form of harm. These issues are considered respectively in Chapters 3 and 4.

ESSENTIAL STEPS IN ESTABLISHING LIABILITY FOR UNINTENTIONAL HARM

First it is necessary to consider the circumstances. Liability in some circumstances is governed by a specific statutory regime. This does not necessarily mean that an action cannot be pursued at common law, but some statutory regimes impose strict liability which gives the pursuer the considerable advantage of not having to show how the defender is at fault. So, for example, the Consumer Protection Act 1987 imposes strict liability on the manufacturer of goods for injury to person or property caused by a defective product. Where harm is caused by animals a strict liability regime is imposed by the Animals (Scotland) Act 1987. In circumstances that are not governed by the Act an action at common law remains competent in which case fault will have to be proved. A duty of care is imposed on the occupiers of premises by the Occupiers' Liability (Scotland) Act s.2(1). This duty is a duty to take reasonable care so in order to establish liability under the Act the pursuer needs to prove negligence on the part of the defender. Care must be taken when grounding an action on a breach of a duty imposed by statute. Not all statutes contemplate that a breach of duty will give rise to civil liability. These issues are discussed in Chapter 7.

Where there is no special liability regime, liability must be established according to common law rules. The common law stipulates that actionable negligence can only arise in circumstances where the defender owes the pursuer a pre-existing **duty of care**.

If it can be established that the defender did owe the pursuer a duty of care, the next step is to show that the defender breached that duty. In order to do this the abstract concept of duty must be given content. This is achieved by defining the appropriate **standard of care**. The standard of care determines what the defender ought or ought not to have done to guard against the risk in the circumstances. Accordingly, the defender's acts or omissions must be measured against the standard of care. If it can be shown that the degree of care taken by the defender fell short of the appropriate standard then it can be held that they breached their duty.

The next step is to show that the harm complained of arose as a result of the defender's breach of duty. In other words, it is necessary to establish **causation**. The breach and the harm must be sufficiently linked. Even though it can be established that a defender owed a duty of care to the pursuer and that that duty was breached, unless the loss can be factually and legally attributed to that breach, the defender will not be liable in reparation.

Finally, the law will not compensate every loss that arises from a breach of duty. Where causation is established the direct and immediate losses arising from a breach are reparable. Indirect or consequential results of a breach may not be. Losses that are too remote will not be compensated. Thus the rules on **remoteness of damage** have to be considered.

These points will be considered in turn in greater detail.

DEVELOPMENT OF THE DUTY OF CARE

In Scots law the civilian divisions of negligence into *culpa lata* (gross negligence) *culpa levis* (light negligence) and *culpa levissima* (very slight negligence) came to be abandoned over the course of the nineteenth century.

The predominant concept in the modern law of negligence is the duty of care. In 1911 Lord President Dunedin observed in *Clelland v Robb*: "Negligence *per se* will not make liability unless there is first of all a duty which there has been failure to perform through that neglect." The view that negligence consists in the breach of a duty was very well established in Scots law by that time. This is evidenced in the Scots literature and case law of the nineteenth century and the language of duty was used in pleadings in the earliest personal injury cases grounded in negligence during the eighteenth century. Indeed the notion of duty is implicit in Stair's presentation of delictual obligations as "obediential".

The overall tendency during the latter part of the nineteenth century and early part of the twentieth was for negligence in Scots and English law to converge. English law too has viewed negligence in terms of duty since *Heaven v Pender* decided in 1883.

This convergence between the two jurisdictions culminated in the celebrated case of *Donoghue v Stevenson*. Poor Mrs Donoghue allegedly suffered severe gastro-enteritis after a decomposing snail emerged from an opaque bottle of fizzy drink that she was pouring over her ice cream. This may have been ginger beer. Equally, the term "ginger" may have arisen in the generic sense in which it is still used in the West of Scotland. Mrs Donoghue's stomach complaint arose from the fact she had already consumed some of the contents of the bottle.

Mrs Donoghue had no right of action in contract since she had no contract with the manufacturer. Moreover, she had no contract with the cafe owner since the drink had been bought for her by her friend. The House of Lords upheld the view of the Inner House that she had a relevant claim in delict. In a famous passage, Lord Atkin formulated what has become known as the neighbourhood principle:

"You must take reasonable care to avoid acts or omissions which you can reasonably foresee would be likely to injure your neighbour. Who, then, in law, is my neighbour? The answer seems to be— persons who are so closely and directly affected by my act that I ought reasonably to have them in contemplation when I am directing my mind to the acts or omissions which are called into question."

The case of *Donoghue v Stevenson* was of tremendous significance. While Lord Atkin's neighbourhood principle can be seen as more or less restating Scots law as described in 1864 by Guthrie Smith in his *Treatise on Reparation*, Lord Atkin took steps to ensure that this Scottish appeal would make an impact on the law in England. English courts had been reluctant to impose duties in novel circumstances and would only recognise a duty where there was a direct precedent for doing so. This rendered the law inflexible and hampered development. Research by Lord Rodger has shown that Lord Atkin prevailed upon Lord MacMillan, one of two Scottish judges on the bench to re-write his speech in terms of English rather than Scots law and counsel conceded that on the relevant points the laws of Scotland and England were the same.

Since *Donoghue* it has been possible to view the law of negligence as the same in both jurisdictions and decisions of the House of Lords in English cases govern Scots law and vice versa. At the same time important differences in terms of the theory and structure of the law remain. Professors McQueen and Sellar state, in *A History of Private Law in Scotland*:

"[T]he intellectual superstructure of the law in the two systems remained different. Scots law held and continues to hold to the systematics of the law of obligations as laid down by Stair within the general tradition of the *jus commune*. Here there has been no shift towards the common law. If anything, the shift has been in the other direction."

In *Donoghue* Lord Atkin explicitly sought to lay down a general principle of law, the application of which would determine the existence or otherwise of a duty of care whenever loss was caused unintentionally. As Lord MacMillan observed: "The categories of negligence are never closed".

The neighbourhood principle in *Donoghue* sets out criteria for determining whether a duty is owed based on foreseeability of harm. If I am going to do something and I can reasonably contemplate that my actions will have a direct effect on you or your property, then I owe you a duty to take care in how I conduct my activities so that I do not cause you harm. If I can, or ought to foresee that my activities might harm you, then I owe you a duty. I should not conduct my activities in disregard of your interests.

Donoghue has proved a fertile ground of legal development, however the case has had its detractors and Lord Atkin's neighbourhood principle does have the potential to expand liability for unintentional harm beyond the boundaries that are considered appropriate. There is an underlying policy concern in negligence that the scope of liability must be restricted. As Cardozo J. expressed the point in *Ultramares Corporation v Touche*, it is necessary to avoid: "liability in an indeterminate amount for an indeterminate time, to an indeterminate class." Negligent acts are not intended to harm and justice requires some equation between the degree of culpability and the extent of liability.

Donoghue allowed for the expansion of liability for unintentional harm into areas such as liability for the acts of third parties, in *Dorset Yacht Co v Home Office* and for pure economic loss, in *Hedley Byrne v Heller and Partners*. These cases will be discussed later.

The expansion of *Donoghue* style liability with foreseeability of harm as the governing criteria reached its zenith in the House of Lords case *Anns v Merton Borough Council* in 1978. Lord Wilberforce proposed a two part test for determining the existence of a duty of care:

> "First one has to ask whether, as between the alleged wrongdoer and the person who has suffered damage there is a sufficient relationship of proximity or neighbourhood such that, in the reasonable contemplation of the former, carelessness on his part may be likely to cause damage to the latter, in which case a *prima facie* duty of care arises. Secondly, if the first question is answered affirmatively, it is necessary to consider whether there are any considerations which ought to negative, or reduce or limit the scope of the duty or the persons to whom it is owed or the damages to which a breach of it may give rise...."

Had this approach found favour it would have meant *prima facie* liability in negligence based firmly on the application of the neighbourhood principle. Liability would then have been confirmed or denied following further considerations such as policy. This further liberalisation of liability in negligence was not well received, particularly since *Anns* occurred in the context of pure economic loss which is a form of harm in which the scope of liability is generally restricted.

Anns was overruled by the House of Lords in *Murphy v Brentwood DC*. It has been observed that since the 1980s the trend in the House of Lords has been to reverse the expansion of liability and the duty of care is used consciously as an instrument to limit the scope of liability. By recognising a duty of care, or by not doing so, courts can exercise control over the scope of liability for unintentional harm. In this sense the duty of care is aptly described as a "threshold device".

While *Donoghue* has allowed for a duty of care to be recognised in a multiplicity of circumstances, in novel circumstances, that is where there is no direct precedent the criteria for recognising a duty of care has been further developed.

In the context of pure economic loss a tripartite test was laid down by the House of Lords in *Caparo Industries plc v Dickman*. First, in order for a duty of care to be recognised harm to the pursuer must be reasonably foreseeable. Secondly, there must be a close degree of proximity between the parties. Thirdly, it must be fair, just and reasonable for the courts to recognise a duty.

This approach maintains existing requirements plus it provides an explicit role for policy considerations in the form of the fair just and reasonable requirement. It is generally applicable where the existence of a duty in novel situations is considered and is not restricted to pure economic loss cases. Indeed, in the context of pure economic loss the *Caparo* approach has been superseded by *Henderson v Merrett Syndicates Ltd*. The application of the *Caparo* requirements can be seen, for example, in the context of personal injury in *Gibson v Chief Constable of Strathclyde*; in the context of property harm in *Marc Rich & Co AG v Bishop Rock Marine Co Ltd*; and in the context of economic loss arising from wrongful birth in *McFarlane v Tayside Health Board*.

ESTABLISHING THE DUTY OF CARE: TO WHOM IS A DUTY OWED?

A duty of care is not owed to the whole world. It is not enough for liability to say that a reasonable person ought to have contemplated that their negligent conduct could have harmed somebody. The pursuer in particular has to be someone whom the defender ought to have contemplated, otherwise there is no duty. The field of potential pursuers is limited by the requirement of proximity.

So, for instance, in *Bourhill v Young* the pursuer's case failed. A fishwife claimed that she had suffered nervous shock resulting in miscarriage when she heard the sound of a collision between a motorcycle and a car and later saw blood on the road. While it was clear that the negligent motorcyclist owed a duty of care to other road users and pedestrians in the vicinity, Mrs Bourhill was at the far side of a tram when the accident occurred and was placed in no danger herself. The motorcyclist could not have foreseen injury to a pedestrian who was so far from events and so the action failed for lack of proximity. Mrs Bourhill herself was outwith the geographical area within which a duty of care was owed.

Similarly in *Hill v Chief Constable of West Yorkshire* the mother of the final victim of Peter Sutcliffe, the Yorkshire Ripper, sued in negligence. It was alleged that the police were negligent in failing to identify and apprehend Sutcliffe prior to the murder of Jacqueline Hill. Indeed, it was admitted by the police that they had made mistakes during the process of investigation. The case was unsuccessful. While it was reasonably foreseeable that young women in general in the Leeds area were in danger while the Ripper remained at large, no duty of care was owed to Jacqueline Hill in particular. This case also involved a policy consideration. It was felt that the admission of an actionable duty of care in such circumstances would have a detrimental effect on the conduct of police operations.

Hill was distinguished in *Gibson v Chief Constable of Strathclyde*. In that case police officers had been guarding a bridge which had collapsed. They had parked their Land Rover at one end of the bridge with the blue light flashing and the headlamps on so that anyone approaching from either end would be warned of the danger. They left without being aware of whether any alternative warning had been established and the next vehicle to approach the bridge fell into the river. It was held that a duty of care was owed to the occupants of the vehicle. The distinction drawn between *Hill* and *Gibson* lies in the different nature of the functions performed by police. The policy considerations that argue against civil liability arising from the investigation of crime do not apply when the emergency services exercise a civil function in assuming control in hazardous road conditions. Having taken control of the situation the police officers were in a sufficiently proximate relationship with other road users for a duty to arise.

The most important distinction between *Hill* and *Gibson* is that in *Hill* the victim was a member of a very wide and barely determinate class of persons whereas in *Gibson* the occupants of the vehicle belonged to a narrowly defined and determinate class. In essence the requirement of proximity means that the pursuer must either be a particular person whom the defender ought to hold in reasonable contemplation or must be within a relatively narrow class of persons. The requirement of proximity effectively narrows the scope of the neighbourhood principle.

ESTABLISHING BREACH OF DUTY: THE STANDARD OF CARE

Establishing a duty of care is only the first step in an action based on negligence. Next it has to be established that the duty was breached. This raises the issue, how much care was the defender obliged to exercise? The defender will only be liable to make reparation if it can be shown that the care taken was less than that required by law. In other words the defender's conduct must have fallen short of that necessary to fulfil the duty. The abstract concept of duty of care is given content by the standard of care. It is up to pursuers to stipulate exactly what the duty was, what the defender should have or should not have done, and to specify the way in which their conduct deviated from the standard required.

The standard of care imposed by law is that of the reasonable man, or ordinarily careful person. So a defender will only be liable if their conduct showed less care than would have been exercised by a reasonable person in the position of the defender at the time at which the event occurred. The standard of the reasonable man is an objective standard and courts will not enquire too deeply into the idiosyncrasies of the individual. Thus a learner driver owes the same standard of care to other road users as an experienced driver (*Nettleship v Weston*). If this seems harsh on the learner driver, the point is that other road users and pedestrians are entitled to expect a certain degree of care, not differing standards according to the experience or lack of it of the driver.

It is important to note that the standard of care is a flexible concept. The degree of care required by law varies according to the circumstances. Some activities require a level of care that is little more than mundane, for example, applying the handbrake when parking a car. Other activities require the most elaborate precautions, open heart surgery or nuclear fission, for example.

The point was put well by Lord Neaves in *Chalmers v Dixon*. "No prudent man in carrying a lighted candle through a powder magazine would fail to take more care than if he was going through a damp cellar." As Lord MacMillan stated in *Muir v Glasgow Corporation*: "There is no absolute standard, but it may be said generally that the degree of care required varies directly with the risk involved."

ESTABLISHING BREACH OF DUTY: THE CALCULUS OF RISK

Ultimately, courts will determine what precautions a reasonable person in the defender's position ought to take or the level of care that ought to be exercised. This determination has been assisted by the identification of factors that ought to be taken into consideration in assessing risk. The most relevant considerations are the likelihood of the risk of harm materialising and the magnitude of the harm if the risk does materialise. This aspect of the law of negligence may be explained most clearly in the context of accidents at work, a situation in which the existence of a duty of care is clear.

It has been held that there is a duty on employers to weigh on the one hand, the magnitude of risk, the likelihood of an accident happening and the possible gravity of any accident against, on the other hand, the difficulty, expense and disadvantage of taking any particular precaution. This balancing process is termed "the calculus of risk". While these factors derive from the judgement of Lord Reid in *Morris v West Hartlepool Steam Navigation Co Ltd* and are commonly illustrated by reference to other employment cases, the basic approach of weighing up the risks against the practicability of precautions is not restricted to the employment field.

In *Brisco v Secretary of State for Scotland* a prison officer sought damages of £2,000 in respect of a broken bone in his little toe, sustained when a heavy fence post thrown from above landed on him during a simulated riot. The pursuer contended that his employers were in breach of their duty to him in failing to issue an instruction forbidding the throwing of heavy objects. In the Inner House the factors outlined in the previous paragraph were considered. In the light of the need for riot training of prison officers under realistic circumstances the instruction contended for by the pursuer would have amounted to a disadvantage.

This disadvantage was sufficient to outweigh the relatively slight risk involved. Accordingly there was no breach of duty.

In *Latimer v AEC Ltd* a factory floor became slippery after flooding. Three tons of sawdust was put down on the floor, but the plaintiff slipped on an uncovered part of the floor and was injured. He argued that the factory should have been closed down. The House of Lords held that the employer had done all that a reasonable employer would have done. Closing down the factory would have meant a loss of production and the expense and disadvantage of this was not outweighed by the relatively small danger to which the plaintiff had been exposed.

A further means of contending for a particular standard of care is to show that defenders have not followed usual practice. The House of Lords decision in *Brown v Rolls Royce* demonstrates that failure to adopt a normal practice is not conclusive proof of negligence, but merely a fact from which negligence may be inferred. The plaintiff contracted dermatitis. He was a machine oiler whose hands were constantly in contact with oil. Evidence was led to show that it was common practice for employers to provide Rozalex #1, a barrier cream. Rolls Royce had not done so, but they had sought medical advice on the issue and contended that Rozalex was not an effective prophylactic. They had made alternative provision in the form of adequate washing facilities. Rolls Royce was not in breach. They had not neglected to take precautions, but had considered the issue, made provision and had demonstrated the conduct and judgment of a reasonable employer. Thus, normal practice may be of evidential value, but will not, in itself, determine the issue.

In *Paris v Stepney Borough Council* it was not at the time usual practice to supply goggles to employees doing the work of the plaintiff. However this employee had been blinded in one eye during the war. When he lost his sight completely through an accident at work that would have been prevented had he been supplied with goggles, his employers were held in breach of their duty to him. This is an example in which the potential magnitude of harm is great given special attributes of the individual owed a duty. Accordingly, a standard of care which is higher than that which operates for other individuals is justified.

ESTABLISHING BREACH OF DUTY: LIKELIHOOD OF INJURY

The duty of care involves the requirement to guard against risks that are likely to materialise, but not against all eventualities. One is only liable for consequences that a reasonable person in the position of the defender would have contemplated in the circumstances when they occurred.

As Lord Oaksey explained:

"The standard of care in the law of negligence is the standard of an ordinary careful man, but in my opinion an ordinary careful man does not take precautions against every foreseeable risk. He can, of course, foresee the possibility of many risks, but life would be almost impossible if he were to attempt to take precautions against every risk which he can foresee. He takes precautions against risks which are reasonably likely to happen. Many foreseeable risks are extremely unlikely to happen and cannot be guarded against except by almost complete isolation".

The context for these remarks was the English House of Lords case of *Bolton v Stone*. In that case a cricket ball was struck right out of a cricket ground where it injured a person around one hundred yards from the wicket. While the event was foreseeable, balls had been struck out of the ground 6 times in the previous 30 years, the defendants who operated the cricket ground were not obliged to have guarded against it. The risk of injury was so remote that a reasonable person would not have anticipated it.

A similar issue was determined by the House of Lords in the earlier Scottish case of *Muir v Glasgow Corporation*. Participants in a Sunday school picnic in King's Park, Glasgow sought shelter from the rain in a tea-room run by the Corporation. The Corporation's employee on the premises, Mrs Alexander, gave permission for the picnic and allowed an urn full of boiling water to be carried down a passageway to the tea-room. The urn was dropped in the passageway scalding several children who were queuing to buy sweeties. The Corporation was sued in negligence.

While it was held that Mrs Alexander owed a duty of care to the children she was not in breach of that duty. The spillage was not foreseeable as a reasonable and probable consequence of her conduct in allowing the urn to be carried. She was entitled to assume that the carriers would have been reasonably careful. With the benefit of hindsight we can see that spillage was a possibility, but the Court deemed that Mrs Alexander would not have foreseen the event as a possibility let alone a probability.

The extent of liability is limited by taking a practical approach. Foreseeability is relevant, not only to establishing the existence of a duty, but also to determining whether the defender's conduct constitutes a breach. *Bolton v Stone* illustrates the point that foreseeability of harm is a necessary, but not a sufficient requirement for breach of duty. For a duty to be breached the conduct complained of must have as its reasonable and probable consequence harm to the pursuer.

Bolton v Stone may be contrasted with the case of *Lamond v Glasgow Corporation* in which a golf ball was hit onto a footpath where it struck the pursuer on the head. In that case the duty of care was breached since the event was not only possible, but also probable. It was established in evidence that on average six thousand golf balls were played onto the footpath every year although there was no previously reported instance of anybody having been struck. Similarly in *Whitefield v Barton* the operators of a golf course were found liable when a wayward tee shot damaged a car. It was found that balls not infrequently went onto the road when struck from this particular tee and the defenders were aware of this. The golfer whose shot caused the damage was assoilzied.

The House of Lords decision in *Hughes v Lord Advocate* demonstrates a very important point. Although the precise way in which an accident occurs may not be reasonably foreseeable, if some accident of that type or general nature is foreseeable then liability may be established. This case involved a hole in the road, covered with a tent, but otherwise insufficiently guarded. Boys investigated with a paraffin lamp that had been marking the road works. The lamp was knocked down the hole. This ignited gas and caused an explosion that burned one of the boys badly. It was held that the explosion was not foreseeable. However it was foreseeable that a child might enter the tent with a lamp, that paraffin might spill and that the child might be burned. Therefore the duty of care owed to pedestrians was breached.

Similarly in *Wilson v Chief Constable of Lothian and Borders Police* a man died of hypothermia having been released by police in a drunken condition in an isolated place at 5.45 on a January morning. It had been snowing heavily, the temperature was 0 degrees. The body was found a week later 2.2 miles from the site of release. It was held that the police were not bound to have foreseen the man's death from hypothermia, but they should have foreseen that he would be exposed to various risks of severe harm. They were under a particular duty to have regard to the reasonably foreseeable consequences of his release. The officers concerned had failed to direct their minds to the likely consequences of their act and had exposed the deceased to unnecessary risk. The chain of events that was foreseeable was not different in kind from those that led to his death.

ESTABLISHING BREACH OF DUTY: SUMMARY

In summary, once the existence of a duty of care is established the onus is on the pursuer to establish that the duty has been breached. In pleadings the pursuer must aver the standard of care applicable. The pursuer will argue that the defender exercised less care than was called for in the circumstances, that is, that the defender's acts or omissions fell short of the appropriate standard. The degree of care that ought to be exercised will vary according to the nature of the activity that gave rise to the harm. Activities that are inherently hazardous require more care than activities where the risk to others is slight. Liability arises only in respect of events that are the reasonable and probable consequence of the breach. The precise details of the harmful incident do not have to be foreseeable so long as an event of that nature or type ought to have been foreseen.

CAUSATION

It is necessary to show that the harm complained of resulted from the defender's breach. A causal link must be established. It must be shown by the pursuer that "but for" the breach, the loss would not have occurred. Thus in *McWilliams v Sir Archibald Arrol & Co*, employers were in breach of their duty since they failed to provide a steel erector with a safety belt. However, they were not liable when he plunged to his death since it was established in evidence that even if he had been given a belt, the steel erector would not have worn it. Similarly in *McKinlay v British Steel Corporation* the pursuer claimed that he had not been instructed and encouraged to wear safety goggles in accordance with the duty on the defenders. On the evidence it was held that the pursuer had failed to establish that he would have worn goggles if instructed to do so. The defenders were assoilzied. In *Barnett v Chelsea and Kensington Hospital Management Committee* the casualty officer was in breach of duty in failing to see a patient who presented with violent vomiting. The patient died later of arsenic poisoning. The hospital was not liable despite the breach, because it was established that the patient would have died anyway. His death was not attributable to the doctor's breach of duty.

So the breach must be the factual cause of the loss. This is expressed as the *causa sine qua non*. This is a necessary, but not sufficient basis for establishing causation. In order to establish causation it is also necessary to establish that the breach is the *causa causans*. That is, the breach must be the legal cause in the sense of being the effective, dominant or immediate cause. Of course, in many circumstances the factual and legal cause are the same, the issue only arises where there are complications in the causal chain. Such complications arise, for example, where there are further acts by the pursuer or by third parties which have some effect on the victim.

The difficulties associated with causation have been exercising the minds of lawyers for a rather long time. This is illustrated by the following passage from Roman Law that will enable the distinction between *causa sine qua non* and *causa causans* to be illustrated.

> "Celsus writes that if one attacker inflicts a mortal wound on a slave and another person later finishes him off, he who struck the earlier blow will not be liable for a killing, but for wounding, because he actually perished as a result of another wound". (D.9.2.11.3.)

The original wound is a *causa sine qua non*, since "but for" the wound the slave might not have been lying around in a position where he could be wounded again. So the original wound is the factual cause. However, the original wound is not the *causa causans*. The *causa causans* is the second attack that kills the slave. The second attack is the effective, dominant or immediate cause of death. The second attack is a *novus actus interveniens* (new act intervening) which breaks the chain of causation between the infliction of the original wound and death, relieving the original wrongdoer from liability.

In *McKew v Holland & Hannon & Cubitts (Scotland) Ltd* the pursuer injured his ankle as a result of the defenders' negligence. His leg thereafter was liable to "give way" on occasions. After the accident he went to visit a flat. Access to the flat was by way of a stair with no handrail. The pursuer descended the stairway without care, his leg gave way, he panicked and jumped down ten steps causing further injury to his leg. The court held the defenders liable for the original injury, but not the second. By descending the stairs without care the pursuer's own act constituted a *novus actus interveniens*. The defenders' breach was a *causa sine qua non* of the second injury, but it was not the *causa causans*.

A further complicating factor arises where there may be more than one cause for the harm suffered. In *Wardlaw v Bonnington Castings* the pursuer contracted pneumoconiosis from breathing in dust at work. The dust might have come from the hammer that he operated for which there was no known means of providing protection and therefore no breach of duty on the part of the employers. Equally the dust might have come from grinders and other machinery for which protection could have been, but was not provided. Accordingly employers were not in breach in respect of one possible source, but were in breach in respect of the other. The House of Lords held that the pursuer could succeed in negligence if he could show that dust from the source for which the defenders were in breach had materially contributed to his injuries. In this case the "but for" test was relaxed.

In *Wardlaw* the potential sources of harm operated concurrently. In the subsequent House of Lords case of *McGhee v National Coal Board* the point was extended to cover sources operating consecutively. In that case also there were two possible sources of harm, one of which involved breach of duty and the other did not. The pursuer worked in a kiln and was exposed to dust. There was no means of effecting protection and therefore no breach of duty. The defenders had failed to supply washing facilities which was a breach of duty and so the pursuer cycled home from work everyday in a generally dusty condition. Again it was impossible to determine whether it was the exposure to dust or the lack of washing facilities that was the effective cause of the pursuer's dermatitis. The pursuer may have contracted dermatitis purely through his work or it might have been that there would have been no harm had he been able to clean up before going home. In this case the "but for" test was abandoned altogether, and it was held that the pursuer could succeed if the breach had materially contributed to the *risk* of harm.

In *Fairchild v Glenhaven Funeral Services* the House of Lords developed further the law on causation. The pursuer contracted mesothelioma as a consequence of exposure to asbestos dust. The complicating factor in this case was that he had been exposed to asbestos while working for two different employers at different times and over different periods. Both parties were in breach, but it was impossible to attribute the source of the disease to a particular employer or a particular period of employment. In this case the "but for" test was suspended. Since the risk of mesothelioma increases with total exposure to asbestos, both employers had materially contributed to the risk and both were found liable.

It appears that where there are two potential sources of harm from the same noxious agent, a material increase in risk may be treated as a material contribution and causation may be established on this basis. The sources need not operate concurrently. Where more than one party is responsible for the material increase in risk all parties in breach may be found liable.

REMOTENESS OF DAMAGE

Where loss occurs there may be no end to the consequences. Imagine I am knocked off my motorbike by the negligence of a car driver while on my way to a job interview. I can seek reparation in respect of my physical injuries both in terms of pain and suffering and any disability I sustain. But my loss does not end there. Because I am in hospital when I was scheduled to be at the interview I do not get the new job, I have to continue in my present job that pays far less. My family suffers financially and eventually my marriage breaks down due to financial strains. Such losses would be regarded as too speculative to be reparable. After all, I may have failed the interview.

A line has to be drawn somewhere between consequences which the negligent defender must bear and those which must be borne by the victim. Thus we have the concept of remoteness of damage. The law will not compensate damage that is too remote.

Historically there has been some difficulty in identifying the criteria applied in Scots law to determine which losses are too remote. It is common to cite a dictum of Lord Kinloch in *Allan v Barclay*:

> "The grand rule on the subject of damages is that none can be claimed except such as naturally and directly arise out of the wrong done; and such therefore, as may reasonably be supposed to have been in the view of the wrongdoer."

This equates direct consequences with those that are reasonably foreseeable. In the past this has caused some difficulty since in English cases direct and reasonably foreseeable consequences have been distinguished and there is conflicting authority to support either view. In *Re Polemis v Furniss Withy & Co Ltd* the Court of Appeal unequivocally rejected foreseeability as the test whereas in *Overseas Tankship (UK) Ltd v Morts Dock and Engineering Co Ltd (The Wagon Mound No.1)* the Privy Council rejected the *Polemis* approach holding that in order to be recoverable, the damage had to be a reasonably foreseeable consequence of the defendant's negligence.

The matter appears to have been resolved in an appeal to the House of Lords in a Scottish case, *Simmons v British Steel plc*. Lord Rodger summarised the law in five points:

1. Once liability is established in terms of duty and breach the starting point is that the defender is not to be held liable for consequences that are not reasonably foreseeable.

2. However the defender is not necessarily liable for all consequences that are reasonably foreseeable. Depending on circumstances there may be no liability for harm resulting from a *novus actus interveniens*, or from unreasonable conduct by the pursuer even if that was foreseeable.

3. Subject to 2. above there will be liability for harm of a kind that was foreseeable even though the harm is greater than could have been foreseen or where it was caused in a way that could not have been foreseen, as, for example, in *Hughes v Lord Advocate*.

4. Subject to 2. above the defender takes his victim as he finds him, so, for example, in *McKillen v Barclay Curle* liability was established not only in respect of the pursuer's fractured rib, but also for consequent reactivation of the pursuer's tuberculosis which the defender could not have foreseen.

5. Subject to 2. above where personal injury is a foreseeable consequence of negligence the defender is liable whether the injury is physical or psychiatric, as in *Page v Smith* discussed below in Chapter 4.

Simmons v British Steel plc makes clear that the governing criteria on remoteness of damage is foreseeability while noting in point 2. that even foreseeable consequences may not be reparable where there has been a break in the chain of causation. There remains much scope for flexibility and argument. The line to be drawn between losses that are reparable and those that are merely speculative will vary according to the circumstances of the particular case.

LIABILITY FOR THE ACTS OF THIRD PARTIES

Outwith circumstances in which vicarious liability operates, one is in general not liable for the deliberate acts of third parties. Normally any such act would constitute a *novus actus interveniens* breaking the chain of causation between the defender's breach and the pursuer's loss. Liability in negligence in such circumstances is very much the exception rather than the rule.

In *Dorset Yacht Co v Home Office* the House of Lords found in favour of the owners of a yacht damaged when borstal boys under the control of prison officers attempted to escape from an island in Poole harbour. Critical to the decision was the view that the prison officers had a supervisory role over the boys, some of whom had a record of absconding and the escape ought to have foreseen. Since the officers knew of the presence of the yacht, and that the yacht offered the only feasible means of escape, they should have foreseen the events that transpired. The boys escaped, commandeered the yacht and there was a collision. The officers owed a duty of care to the owners of the yacht since they ought to have foreseen harm to their property as the result of the negligent way in which they exercised their supervisory role. They had gone to bed and left the boys to their own devices.

This case can be seen as an extension of the duty of care to cover acts by third parties, but it can be rationalised, as Lord Reid did in his speech, in terms of causation. An act of a third party need not necessarily be seen as a *novus actus interveniens*, especially where, in a case such as this, the third party is under the control of the negligent party. Even though the harm occurred through voluntary actions on the part of the boys, these actions were foreseeable to the negligent prison officers.

Liability for the acts of third parties has also been considered in the context of whether there is a duty owed to neighbours in respect of damage caused by persons entering the pursuer's property. In *Evans v Glasgow DC* the neighbourhood principle from *Donoghue* was applied to hold landlords liable for property damage in a tenement caused by vandals who had entered adjoining vacant property. The defenders were negligent in failing to secure the vacant property against a foreseeable risk. In 1986 the case of *Squires v Perth & Kinross District Council* was determined in the Inner House. The second defenders, a firm of building contractors, were found liable in negligence having breached a duty of care owed to the pursuers to secure premises against access by third parties. The builders had been carrying out renovation work on flats above the pursuers' premises, a jewellers shop. A thief had gained access to one of the flats which was not properly secured and had broken through the floor into the shop below.

The Court held that this was an event that ought to have been foreseen and guarded against. As Lord Wheatley said: "Any reasonable person in occupancy and control would have foreseen the likelihood of what in fact occurred".

The following year the case of *Maloco v Littlewoods* (also reported *sub nom. Smith v Littlewoods*) was decided in the House of Lords. The defenders owned an empty cinema, the Regal in Dunfermline. Children broke in and started fires which damaged neighbouring property. The House of Lords held that there was no breach of any duty owed to neighbouring proprietors.

Lord McKay, a Scottish judge, appeared to determine the case on the ground that the event that transpired was not foreseeable. The defenders did not know of previous acts of vandalism involving fire. Since the cinema was not an obvious fire risk the defenders were not under a duty to anticipate the possibility of fire by vandals.

However, the decision in *Maloco* may be better explained as following the English Court of Appeal case of *Perl Exporters v Camden LBC*. In that case the defendants were held to owe no duty to neighbours to secure their property, despite the fact that they had been made well aware of the accessibility of the property to vagrants and of the concerns of the plaintiffs regarding security. When thieves broke through the adjoining wall and stole garments belonging to the plaintiffs, Perl sued in negligence. Notwithstanding the manifest carelessness of the defendants it was held that no duty of care was owed.

Lord Goff stated:

> "Is every occupier of a terraced house under a duty to his neighbours to shut his windows or lock his door when he goes out, or to keep access to his cellars secure, or even to remove his fire escape, at the risk of being held liable in damages if thieves thereby obtain access to his own house and thence to his neighbour's house? I cannot think that the law imposes any such duty."

The point is that English law demonstrates great reluctance to recognise a duty of care in respect of a pure omission. English law imposes no duty on proprietors to secure their property against third parties even though it is foreseeable that such persons may use their access to the property to cause harm to neighbouring properties. In *Perl* and *Maloco* it was not any positive act on the part of the defending parties that was complained of, but a failure to act in circumstances where the law recognises no duty to act.

Since *Maloco* is a decision of the House of Lords in a Scottish case there is little scope for doubting that this is also the law of Scotland. It may be that whether harm is foreseeable is beside the point. The point being that the law imposes no duty to secure one's property to protect one's neighbours. Nevertheless in one subsequent case, *Fry's Metals Ltd v Durastic Ltd* tenants were liable in delict to their landlords when vandals caused damage to the building after the lease had expired and the tenant's own security system had been deactivated. There are a number of curious features to this case, but it may be noted that here the harm was to the unsecured property itself and not to neighbouring property.

WRONGFUL BIRTH AND CONCEPTION

Within the last 20 years there has been a number of actions brought against doctors and their employers in respect of the birth of unplanned or unwanted children. The general tendency has been to admit such claims.

Such a claim may arise from the failure of hospital staff to warn a pregnant mother of potential physical or mental impairment in the foetus so that the mother is denied the opportunity to terminate the pregnancy. This is wrongful birth. It is established that a duty of care to inform the mother is owed in such circumstances. If the duty is breached, damages will be recoverable. The Scots case of *McLelland v Greater Glasgow Health Board* follows the earlier decision of the Court of Appeal in *McKay v Essex Area Health Authority*.

Another way in which such claims arise is where a sterilisation has been performed negligently or, more pertinently, where the patient has been negligently informed that the operation has been a success when it was not. This is wrongful conception. Unwanted pregnancy and childbirth is held to be reparable loss.

While the moral aspects of regarding the birth of a child as a loss provide scope for discussion, the legal point with which we are concerned here is the extent of recovery in damages. This was ruled upon by the House of Lords in the case of *McFarlane v Tayside Health Board*. In *McFarlane* the male pursuer, a father of four, underwent a vasectomy and was subsequently given the "all clear" whereas in fact the operation had been unsuccessful. Subsequently his wife conceived a fifth child. The McFarlanes sued, seeking solatium in respect of pain, suffering and inconvenience consequential on pregnancy and childbirth and damages in respect of the financial costs of bringing up the child.

At first instance the Lord Ordinary, (Lord Gill) accepted that a duty of care was owed the parents, but refused to countenance either the birth of a healthy child as a reparable loss or pregnancy and childbirth as personal injury. On reclaiming the Second Division reversed this decision. Unplanned conception was held to amount to a loss and the McFarlanes were awarded both solatium and damages in respect of financial costs of upbringing.

The defenders appealed to the House of Lords on the basis that natural processes of conception and childbirth could not in law amount to personal injury. This argument was rejected and the mother's claim for solatium was allowed by a majority (Lord Millet dissenting). It was accepted therefore that unplanned conception amounted to a wrong. However, the claim for financial costs was rejected unanimously. This loss was treated as economic loss. The Court determined that it would not be fair, just and reasonable to impose liability on the defenders in respect of such financial costs. In other words, as it has been put by one commentator, "doctors and the NHS are not to pay for the upbringing of healthy children." On the other hand it has been argued, by Professor Thomson that treating such costs as purely economic is wrong in principle. The costs of bringing up the child are consequent on the original delict. Since, in cases of wrongful conception the parties' interest in limiting the size of their family is recognised as a reparable interest it follows that associated costs are derivative and not pure.

The question that arose following *McFarlane*, in which the child was born healthy was whether damages would be recoverable for the costs of upbringing in the event that a child was born with some impairment. In *McLelland v Greater Glasgow Health Board* damages were awarded in respect of the extra costs of maintenance attributable to mental impairment. However this does not answer the point since in this case the wrong consisted of a negligent failure to diagnose mental impairment *in utero* thus denying the mother to choice of whether to proceed with the pregnancy. Thus it was a case of wrongful birth rather than wrongful conception and it has been argued that the two may be distinguished.

Subsequently in *Parkinson v St James and Seacroft University NHS Trust* the claimant was awarded damages in the Court of Appeal, not for the basic costs of upbringing but for the extra costs of raising an autistic child. This was a case of negligently performed sterilisation and therefore wrongful conception.

More recently in a further wrongful conception case *Rees v Darlington Memorial Hospital* the Court of Appeal awarded a mother damages in respect of the extra costs consequent upon the mother's visual impairment of bringing up a healthy child. This decision was reversed in the House of Lords. Ultimately the mother was awarded damages in respect of pregnancy and childbirth as *per McFarlane*. In addition she was awarded a "conventional sum" of £15,000. This sum is awardable in all cases where birth follows failed sterilisation. The conventional payment is itself controversial.

Rees, like *McFarlane* was determined on a majority. The issues remain highly controversial and the law should not yet be regarded as fully settled.

DEFENCES

In general the pursuer's pleadings may be attacked at any point. In defence it may be argued that: no duty of care was owed the pursuer; the appropriate standard of care was exercised; the alleged harm was not caused by the pursuer; the alleged loss was too remote. Note that the facts averred by the pursuer may also be challenged. The defender may be able to establish in proof a very different version of events. The defender may challenge the extent of harm averred by the pursuer.

Over and above any such attack on fundamental aspects of the pursuer's case, the defender may argue that the pursuer contributed to their losses. This is a plea of contributory negligence. In personal injury cases such a plea is more or less routine. It must be established that the pursuer was at fault in that their act or omission fell below the standard of a reasonable person in the pursuer's position. A common example is where a passenger in a car is injured as a result of the driver's negligence, but injuries are exacerbated, because the passenger has failed to wear a seatbelt.

The effect of a successful plea of contributory negligence is to reduce the sum payable in damages by an amount to reflect the degree of the pursuer's own contribution to the harm sustained (Law Reform (Contributory Negligence) Act 1945, s.1). Prior to the 1945 Act contributory negligence was a complete defence, exonerating the defender entirely from the obligation to make reparation.

Where contribution is established courts apportion blame for the damage between the parties and seek to effect a reduction in damages that is just and equitable. For example, in *Sayers v Harlow UDC* damages were reduced by 25 per cent to reflect the plaintiff's own contribution to her injuries. She had been trapped in a public toilet cubicle, but in attempting to climb out was held to have contributed to her losses. Her foot slipped on the toilet roll holder and she fell to the floor.

In reducing damages courts must determine the total damages that would have been awarded had there been no contribution by the defender. Thus we can see the exact apportionment of blame determined by the court. In *Campbell v Gillespie* a mechanic was working at night on a broken down lorry on the A87 between Shiel Bridge and Kyle of Lochalsh. This road is fast in places and it is not lit. The lorry's lights had been disconnected and the mechanic should have provided protection by parking his own, lit vehicle behind the lorry. There was a police warning sign and other vehicles had avoided the lorry before the pursuer's husband ploughed into the back of it at 60 mph or faster in his Vauxhall Astra. The car driver was held 60 per cent to blame, the mechanic, 40 per cent.

A further defence is afforded by the doctrine of *volenti non fit injuria* (to one consenting no wrong is done). *Volenti* operates where it can be held that the pursuer has consented to the risk undertaken by the defender. The defender must establish that the pursuer had knowledge of the risk and willingly assented to it. *Volenti* is a complete defence. Where established it relieves the defender from all liability. The defence of *volenti* does not apply to passengers in road vehicles (Road Traffic Act 1988, s.149). Thus a claim against an over enthusiastic driver who has crashed cannot be defeated by arguing that the passenger should have asked to leave the vehicle when the dangerous nature of the driving first became apparent. Drivers must by law have third party insurance cover. Where there is no such cover the Motor Insurance Bureau will step in and meet established claims. No such restriction applies to aircraft. In *Morris v Murray* two friends took off in a light aircraft following an afternoon's heavy drinking. The plane crashed shortly after take off and the injured passenger sued the pilot's estate. The defence of *volenti* was successfully established.

It should be noted that *volenti* is not restricted in scope to negligence actions, but is a generally available defence in delict. For example, in the assault case of *Reid v Mitchell* it was argued that the pursuer was *volens* of the risk of falling off the haycart. The defence did not succeed since it was held that the pursuer was not a willing participant in the general larking about.

---

3. LIABILITY FOR UNINTENTIONALLY CAUSED FINANCIAL HARM

The recovery of financial or economic loss in negligence poses difficulties. In order to understand what types of economic loss are recoverable it is first useful to distinguish the different forms such loss may take. Economic loss falls into one of three classifications: derivative, secondary and pure.

Derivative economic loss arises where financial harm follows as a consequence of harm to the person or property of the pursuer. Derivative economic loss is reparable.

Secondary economic loss arises where financial harm follows as a consequence of harm to the person or property of third parties. Secondary economic loss is not reparable.

Pure economic loss arises where the only form of harm suffered is financial and there is no loss in the form of personal injury or property damage. Generally, pure economic loss caused negligently is not recoverable and the loss lies where it falls. However, there are circumstances in which exceptions are made to the general rule.

Economic wellbeing is not an interest that is protected against unintentional harm. Law does not in general impose a duty of care on persons not to cause others economic loss. In fact causing economic loss to others is an integral feature of a market economy where competition operates. If a successful company increases its market share by gaining more customers this may be because it has expanded the market. Equally the company may have won customers from less successful competitors. This is not a legal wrong.

The general rule is that actions to recover pure economic loss may not competently be grounded in negligence. However, where pure economic loss is the result, not of negligence, but of deliberate or intentional wrongful conduct, such as fraud, defamation or wrongful interference with contracts, damages may indeed be recovered. Moreover, economic loss may be recoverable in contract. Of course, this depends upon the existence of a contract between pursuer and defender. Recovery in the circumstances will depend upon the terms of the contract and on contract law on breach and remoteness of damages. In summary, purely economic interests are protected by the law of contract and by the intentional delicts, but not, in general, by the law of negligence.

The distinction between harm to property or person and purely financial harm has come to be viewed as fundamental in the context of unintentional harm. This view was challenged in *Anns v Merton London*

Borough Council, but was affirmed afresh by the House of Lords in *Murphy v Brentwood District Council* in which *Anns* was overruled.

DERIVATIVE LOSSES AND DEFECTIVE PROPERTY

Subject to rules on remoteness of damage financial loss which is a consequence of harm to property or person is recoverable. While such losses may in reality be economic they are not treated as such by the law. Thus, if you injure me, you may be liable in damages not only in respect of my pain and suffering, but also for my loss of earnings and relatives' services or costs of nursing.

If you damage my car through your negligence then you must pay for its repair. The financial costs are derivative of harm to my property. However, some care must be taken when considering goods that are defective from the outset. If an electrical appliance has some latent defect that causes my house to burn down, then the cost of rebuilding my house is derivative economic loss and recoverable, since this is an example of defective property damaging other property. Where defective goods cause injury, this is recoverable in principle although the operative liability regime is now statutory (Consumer Protection Act 1987). However, the cost of repairing or replacing defective goods that do not harm either other property or persons is only recoverable in contract.

The same principles that apply to defective goods also apply to defective buildings. A defect that is not dangerous, such as defective plasterwork, does not amount to property damage, but is treated as a defect in quality. As such the financial consequences of defects in buildings are regarded as pure economic loss. There may be a remedy in contract, but in circumstances where the pursuer has no contract with the plasterer, for example, because the defective work was carried out for a builder by a sub-contractor, recovery will not be possible and the loss will lie where it falls (*D&F Estates Ltd v Church Commissioners for England*). There is an exception which operates in narrow circumstances. This is known as *Junior Books* liability which is discussed below.

To be recoverable damage caused by defective property must be damage caused to other, different property. Thus if a house is built on inadequate foundations, consequent damage to walls in the form of cracking and subsidence is not derivative loss, but there is a defect in the quality of the building which amounts to pure economic loss (*Murphy v Brentwood District Council*).

SECONDARY ECONOMIC LOSS

The rule on secondary economic loss is essentially a rule on remoteness of damages. There is no liability where a person suffers financial loss consequent on harm caused negligently to somebody else or somebody else's property. The rule serves to draw a line under the liability of defenders. Were this not the case, then defenders could be liable to a degree out of all proportion to the extent of their wrongdoing. Moreover, liability could arise in respect of an indeterminate class of potential litigants. Thus in *Reavis v Clan Line Steamers* the pursuer failed to recover losses arising from the death of members of her orchestra when the ship on which they were travelling sank. Her loss arose from her consequent inability to stage performances for which she was contracted. The shipping company, whose negligence was responsible for the deaths were not liable to her for losses arising from the inability of the deceased to fulfil their own contracts with her.

So far as property damage is concerned the leading case in Scots law is *Dynamco v Holland, Hannen & Cubitts*. The pursuers lost production in their factory as the result of a power cut. The defenders had negligently severed a power line. Since the power line was the property of the electricity company and not of the pursuers, the pursuers' losses were secondary and thus not recoverable.

An important point to note is that foreseeability of harm to pursuers is not the issue. This is well illustrated by the case of *East Lothian Angling Association v Haddington Town Council*. The pursuers' economic interests were adversely affected by pollution of the river Tyne by the defenders. The pollution affected fishing that in turn affected the sale of permits. It was averred that since the existence of the pursuers was known to the defenders, a duty of care was owed on the basis of the neighbourhood principle. This argument, like a similar argument posed earlier in *Dynamco*, failed. The fact that the pursuers had no proprietary interest in the subjects affected by the negligent act proved fatal to the claim. This defect could not be made good by any attempt to establish proximity between the parties.

PURE ECONOMIC LOSS

While pure economic loss is in general not recoverable in negligence there are exceptions. Exceptions to the general rule on non-recovery in negligence for pure economic loss may be brought together under one head. There is no duty in negligence to avoid causing financial loss save, in the words of Lord Bridge in *Murphy*: "by reason of some special relationship of proximity which imposes on the tortfeasor a duty of care to protect against economic loss".

Therefore, before a duty of care can be held to lie in respect of pure economic loss, the pursuer must satisfy what have been termed enhanced requirements of proximity.

It is possible to denote three types of circumstance in which courts have recognised a duty of care to protect against pure economic loss. Thus a duty may arise in respect of negligent misstatement following *Hedley Byrne v Heller and Partners*. Negligent solicitors may owe a duty of care to disappointed beneficiaries where wills have been carelessly administered to the pursuers' loss following *White v Jones*. Finally a duty of care may arise following the case of *Junior Books Ltd v Veitchi Co Ltd*.

LIABILITY FOR NEGLIGENT MISSTATEMENT

Heller and Partners was a firm of advertising agents who had done a small amount of work for a client called Easipower. Easipower had plans for a far more extensive advertising campaign. Because there was some doubt regarding the financial position of Easipower, Heller sought a reference from Easipower's bankers, Hedley Byrne via their own bankers, National Provincial. On the strength of the positive reference provided by Hedley Byrne, Heller went ahead and placed adverts for Easipower. Subsequently Easipower went into liquidation leaving Heller with losses arising from their performance of the contract of £17,661.18/10d.

The judge at first instance and the Court of Appeal held that no duty of care was owed Heller by Hedley Byrne. In the House of Lords it was held that a duty of care did arise in the circumstances. However Heller was unable to recover damages, because the reference had been given with a specific disclaimer of responsibility on the part of Hedley Byrne.

In *Hedley Byrne* it was held that a duty of care not to cause economic loss could be recognised in circumstances where there had been an assumption of responsibility on the part of the person making the statement. In addition the pursuer must have relied upon the defender to exercise such a degree of care as the circumstances required. Such reliance must have been reasonable and the defender must have known or ought to have known that the pursuer would rely on the defender's statement.

Hedley Byrne was a landmark decision. This case overruled the earlier decision of the Court of Appeal in *Candler v Crane Christmas & Co* in which it was held that a contractual or fiduciary relationship between the parties was necessary before a duty of care in negligence could arise. *Hedley Byrne* gave effect to Lord Justice Denning's dissenting opinion in *Candler*.

The rule in *Hedley Byrne* has been applied in a number of subsequent cases in which recovery of damages has been allowed in respect of negligent misstatement. For example, in *Esso Petroleum Co v Mardon* the owners of a petrol station made a careless representation to a prospective tenant regarding the potential throughput of petrol. The tenancy was taken in reliance on this statement. In court it was determined that the owners had held themselves out as having special expertise in circumstances which gave rise to a duty of care.

In *Martin v Bell Ingram* it was held that a surveyor, conducting a house survey under a contract with a building society, owes a duty of care to the prospective buyer of the house provided that the surveyor knows the survey report will be used and relied upon by that particular buyer.

Further refinements were made to the law in negligent misstatement in *Caparo Industries plc v Dickman*. Here it was held that a negligently prepared company audit could not be used to found a claim when company shareholders successfully mounted a takeover bid on the strength of audited accounts. The accounts showed a profit of £1.3 million whereas the true figure was a loss of £0.46 million. No duty of care was owed the shareholders as potential investors.

In *Hedley Byrne*, *Esso Petroleum* and *Martin* the party making the statement was aware not only of the identity of the party relying on the statement, but also knew of the particular transaction in respect of which reliance was placed on the statement. In order to satisfy the requirements of proximity, the negligent auditors in *Caparo* would have had to have known that these particular investors would rely on the audit for purposes of their takeover. In *Caparo* the tripartite test outlined in Chapter 2 was laid down. Before a duty could be recognised loss to the pursuer must be reasonably foreseeable and there had to be a sufficient degree of proximity between the parties. *Caparo* made clear that it must have been reasonably foreseeable to the defender that the pursuer would act on the defender's advice or statement in a particular transaction or transaction of a particular type. It must have been be reasonably foreseeable to the defender that if insufficient care was taken in making the statement, loss on the part of the pursuer would result. Moreover, courts would only recognise a duty of care in circumstances where it was fair, just and reasonable to do so.

Caparo rules governed until *Henderson v Merrett Syndicates Ltd*. Since *Henderson* the recognition of a duty of care depends upon a voluntary assumption of responsibility for the economic interests of the party to whom the statement is made. The party making the statement must know that the other party is relying on his skill and expertise. A disclaimer of responsibility may prevent a duty from arising since it negates any inference that may be drawn that there has been an assumption of responsibility.

It appears from *Royal Bank of Scotland plc v Bannerman, Johnstone Maclay* that an assumption of responsibility can be inferred where a statement is made in the knowledge that the pursuer is relying on it. The pursuer need not prove that the defender intended to assume responsibility.

Moreover it may be noted that a disclaimer of responsibility will serve to prevent a duty from arising in the first place whereas under the *Caparo* rules disclaimers did not have this effect, but could negate liability for negligence once that was established. Disclaimers were subject to the reasonableness test imposed by s.16(1) of the Unfair Contract Terms Act 1977. This occurred in *Smith v Eric S Bush* in which the circumstances were similar to *Martin v Bell Ingram*. In *Smith* the disclaimer was held to fail the statutory test of reasonableness in the circumstances. There had been a disclaimer sent in *Martin*, but it had arrived too late to have any effect on legal relations between the parties.

The question arises whether the Unfair Contract Terms Act applies to disclaimers in cases determined under *Henderson* rules. The answer, following *Bank of Scotland v Fuller Peiser*, is yes. Disclaimers that seek to prevent a duty from arising in the first place are subject to the statutory test in the same way as terms that seek to deny liability in the event that negligence is established. The relevant provision is s.25(5).

The facts in *Bank of Scotland v Fuller Peiser* were as follows. A Mrs Mackay sought a valuation survey on a hotel from a firm of surveyors. The Bank of Scotland who was lending the money for the purchase requested the survey directly from the surveyors. The transaction went ahead with the Bank taking out a standard security over the hotel. When Mrs Mackay defaulted on the loan the Bank sold the hotel and the sale did not realise the full extent of the debt. The survey upon which the Bank had relied for valuation of the hotel had been negligently conducted. The Bank sought to recover their losses from the surveyors who relied on a disclaimer sent to Mrs MacKay stating that they "accepted no responsibility to any party other than the client".

The disclaimer suggested that the defenders had no intention of assuming responsibility to the Bank for the accuracy of the survey. Nonetheless, Lord Eassie held that in order to be effective the disclaimer had to pass the reasonableness test under the Unfair Contract Terms Act. Given the circumstances, that the parties were of equal bargaining power and that the Bank could well have afforded to instruct an independent survey the disclaimer was deemed reasonable and so the defenders evaded liability.

Following *Henderson* a duty of care not to cause economic loss has been held to arise in the context of personal references. In these cases persons have been unable to find work following poor references negligently prepared. See, for example, *Spring v Guardian Assurance plc and Donlon Colonial Mutual Group (UK Holdings) Ltd.*

LIABILITY OF SOLICITORS TO DISAPPOINTED BENEFICIARIES

In general a solicitor acting for a client acts under a contract and may be concurrently liable to the client in both contract and delict. However the solicitor owes no duty of care to third parties. Recent developments, not only in English law, but also in Commonwealth jurisdictions, the United States and some civilian countries such as France and Germany show that courts are increasingly willing to modify this position.

In *Ross v Caunters* 1980 the Court of Appeal held that a solicitor owed a duty of care to an identified third party who had been named as beneficiary in a will. Because the will had been negligently executed by the solicitor the beneficiary failed to benefit from the intended legacy. Damages were awarded. The decision in this case owes more to *Donoghue* principles than it does to *Hedley Byrne* since the element of reliance, essential to *Hedley Byrne* liability was not present.

Scots law declined to follow the lead given by *Ross* in 1990 when, in *Weir v JM Hodge & Son* it was held in the Outer House that a duty of care was not owed a disappointed beneficiary in circumstances similar to *Ross*. While it is clear from his opinion that he had some sympathy with the pursuer, Lord Weir considered himself bound by the earlier House of Lords decision in *Robertson v Fleming*. While Scots and English law were for a time out of step the position has changed since the House of Lords case of *White v Jones*. This case has been followed in Scots law in *Holmes v Bank of Scotland*.

In *White* the House of Lords ruled by a majority that disappointed beneficiaries could recover in tort in respect of a will that was not drawn up at all. Following a family dispute the deceased had instructed a will that disinherited his daughters. There was a reconciliation and the solicitor was instructed to draft a new will. The solicitor neglected to do this so that when the testator died the distribution of the estate was governed by the original will. The House of Lords declined to follow *Robertson* which was viewed as out of sympathy with current developments in a number of jurisdictions and *Ross v Caunters* was approved.

There are a number of conceptual difficulties posed by the cases of *Ross* and *White* and these are fully discussed in *White* in the speech of Lord Goff. Nevertheless the current position may be viewed as broadly satisfactory on the grounds that liability extends only to beneficiaries whose existence will of course be known to the solicitor. Thus there is proximity between parties and the scope of liability is not indeterminate.

JUNIOR BOOKS LIABILITY

Finally, the case of *Junior Books Ltd v The Veitchi Co Ltd* must be noted. In *Junior Books* a subcontractor was held liable to the owner of premises in respect of the costs of replacing a defective floor. Despite the fact that the subcontractors had no direct contractual relationship with the owners and the loss was pure economic loss since the defective floor was neither dangerous nor likely to cause harm to persons or other property, the House of Lords allowed recovery of damages.

It was significant to the decision that Veitchi, the subcontractor was nominated by the agent of the Junior Books. Thus Veitchi would have known the identity of the owners and that Junior Books would rely on their skill and expertise. Accordingly they would have known that careless performance on their part would result in economic loss to Junior Books.

It may be noted that *Junior Books* dates from the period when *Anns v Merton Borough Council* was in force. English courts have been reluctant to follow it, but there are a number of subsequent Scots cases including *Scott Lithgow Ltd v GEC Electrical Products Ltd*; *Strathford East Kilbride Ltd v HLM Design Ltd*; and *Comex Houlder Diving Ltd v Colne*

Fishing Co Ltd (No.2). The essential points about *Junior Books* liability are that the parties should be linked by a series of contracts operating at the same time; the defender must know that the pursuer is relying on the exercise of skill and expertise from which it follows that the defender must know who the pursuer is. Loss to the pursuer must be reasonably foreseeable to the defender as a consequence of negligently conducted operations.

These circumstances are readily distinguishable from *D&F Estates* since in that case the work was complete before the plaintiffs entered into their contract of lease. There was never any link through contracts in place at the same time, nor could the defendants have contemplated loss to these particular plaintiffs.

4. MENTAL HARM

INTRODUCTION

The term "nervous shock" is used in some circumstances as an alternative to psychiatric or mental harm. Medically, the expression may be dubious. However, lawyers tend to persist in the term nervous shock as it indicates the way in which courts have approached this phenomenon. This is true historically and the idea of an immediate and overwhelming blow to the senses causing mental harm still informs current legal thinking.

While historically courts have been circumspect about the possibility of spurious claims, modern psychiatry is such that there are physical symptoms that may be more easily faked than mental health problems. The law does indeed demand, for a relevant claim, that pursuers suffer some recognised psychiatric condition such as Post Traumatic Stress Disorder. Following *Simpson v ICI* it is clear that mere anxiety or emotional distress is not sufficient to found a claim.

Finally, it should be noted that there is a growing body of case law involving recovery of damages from employers in respect of stress related illness in the workplace. Such cases follow from *Walker v Northumberland County Council*. This is a related, but different area of liability from that under consideration in this chapter.

RECOGNITION OF THE PRINCIPLE OF RECOVERY

Initially, courts demonstrated much reluctance in recognising non-physical personal injury as reparable. The policy reason for this attitude is made clear through a number of judicial dicta to the effect that admitting such a form of loss would result in a barrage of spurious claims. At one time, loss in the form of psychiatric harm was simply viewed as too remote. Thus, in 1888, in *Victorian Railway Commissioners v Coultas* the Privy Council refused damages to a lady who had suffered "severe nervous shock" and subsequent illness and miscarriage after a very narrow escape from being run down by a train. However, *Coultas* was not followed two years later in *Bell v Great Northern Railway of Ireland*. The Exchequer Division in Ireland awarded damages to a female train passenger who had suffered nervous shock through fear for her own safety. The railway company was held to be in breach of a duty to convey passengers not only safely, but securely.

In 1891 an award of £500 in damages was given in the Court of Session to a man who suffered nervous shock during a freak rail accident (*Wood v North British Railway Co*). A train coming in the other direction carried a load of pit props that protruded beyond the width of the trucks. When the pursuer's train met the goods train the props broke through the carriage in which the pursuer was a passenger and brought his train to a violent halt. This case went to the House of Lords, but the issue there was whether the pursuer was barred from seeking damages in court having accepted an offer in settlement. The House of Lords did not determine an issue of whether nervous shock was reparable until *Bourhill v Young* in 1943. In *Wood* the award made by the Lord Ordinary was not disturbed. Only the English judges appear to have doubted whether such loss was reparable.

That psychiatric harm is recoverable in principle was only clearly established in English law in *Dulieu v White & Sons* although there is an earlier example of damages awarded by the Queen's Bench Division in *Wilkinson v Downton* where the plaintiff was the victim of a joke. This however did not involve negligence. In *Dulieu* the Divisional Court of the Kings Bench Division allowed recovery of damages to a woman who had suffered a severe shock when a horse van was negligently driven into the bar in which she worked. The plaintiff was pregnant at the time and later gave premature birth to a child who, as the law report puts it, was "born an idiot". *Dulieu* was subsequently followed in 1908 in the Scottish case of *Wallace v Kennedy*.

Thus, at the beginning of the twentieth century it was clear that psychiatric harm in the form of nervous shock was not too remote to give rise to recovery in damages. Recovery at the time was restricted to those whose shock was caused by fear for their own personal safety rather than fear for the safety of others. Moreover, damages were recoverable even though nervous shock was unaccompanied by physical injury.

REASONABLE FORSEEABILITY

The first case in which damages were recovered where the victim of shock was concerned, not for her own safety, but for that of her children was *Hambrook v Stokes* in 1925. This was a majority decision of the Court of Appeal. However, the status of *Hambrook* as an authority remained in doubt following *Bourhill v Young*. *Bourhill* emphasised the importance of reasonable foreseeability of psychiatric harm to the pursuer before a duty of care could arise. As Lord Denning said ten years later in *King v Phillips*: "...there can be no doubt since *Bourhill v Young* that the test of liability for shock is foreseeability of injury by shock". In *King* the Court of Appeal denied damages to a mother who had witnessed a taxi driver negligently reversing over her son's tricycle. The plaintiff heard the boy scream from seventy to eighty yards away, but could not see the boy when the taxi stopped. In fact he was unharmed. Ostensibly, like Mrs Bourhill, the plaintiff was too far from the incident for a duty of care to be owed her. The unacknowledged reason for the decision was one of policy. The Court sought to restrict liability for fear of "opening the floodgates" to large number of claims.

In 1967 liability for nervous shock was extended to rescuers. In *Chadwick v British Transport Commission* the plaintiff suffered depression and eventually committed suicide following horrific experiences in aiding victims of the Lewisham train disaster. The view was taken that it was reasonably foreseeable that in such an event, citizens would come to the rescue and so a duty of care was owed those who did. Moreover, the actions of a rescuer do not constitute a *novus actus interveniens* breaking the chain of causation between the negligent act and resultant harm. This is because the rescuer acts out of moral obligation so their involvement is not treated as voluntary. From a policy point of view it was thought undesirable to deny recovery to selfless and altruistic rescuers.

EXTENSION OF PRINCIPLE OF RECOVERY

In 1983 in *McLoughlin v O'Brian* the House of Lords allowed recovery in damages to a mother who witnessed the immediate aftermath of a road accident in which her husband and two children were injured and one child was killed. The limiting principle in *Dulieu*, that the shock must result for fear for personal safety was rejected. The existence of the duty of care owed the plaintiff was based on reasonable foreseeability of psychiatric harm, but the Court was also concerned with policy. In order to limit potential claims it was held necessary to have witnessed the incident or its immediate aftermath directly. Mrs McLauchlin arrived at the hospital where her family were held two hours after the accident. In holding that she witnessed the immediate aftermath it was significant that the victims had not been cleaned up, nor had wounds been dressed.

THE CURRENT POSITION

It has been possible to categorise pursuers in terms of participants, bystanders and rescuers, or in terms of those shocked through fear for their own safety as opposed to those shocked through witnessing horrific events befall others. The critical distinction in the modern context is between primary and secondary victims. This follows from the House of Lords cases of *Page v Smith* and *White v Chief Constable of South Yorkshire*. This distinction is not always easy to draw. Broadly, a primary victim is a person within the range of potential physical harm. A secondary victim is a person outwith the range of potential physical harm.

Thus, new cases have to be approached, not by identifying the pursuer as a participant, bystander or rescuer, but by enquiring whether the pursuer was within the range of potential physical harm. For example, a rescuer might be either a primary or secondary victim depending upon the circumstances. In *White* the respondent police officers had been involved in assisting victims of the Hillsborough disaster. They were not held entitled to damages as they had not been in physical danger themselves. They were not, therefore, primary victims and moreover were unable to satisfy the requirements for recovery of damages demanded of secondary victims. By contrast in *Hale v London Underground* a fireman successfully recovered damages for nervous shock. He had assisted in the Kings Cross disaster while the incident was still occurring. He had been exposed to considerable danger. Subsequently he suffered horrendous nightmares and severe depression. On his return to work he was only able to do a desk job.

PRIMARY VICTIMS

In *Page v Smith* a man suffered a re-occurrence of ME (myalgic encephalomyelitis) when the stationary car in which he was sitting was bumped by the defendant's car. ME was regarded by the Court at the time as a form of mental harm. Research suggests that its provenance as a medical condition is in some doubt. Clearly drivers owe a duty of care to other drivers and pedestrians within the range of potential harm not to cause personal injury or damage their property. However it was arguable that while physical harm might have been reasonably foreseeable, psychiatric harm was not. Nevertheless, damages were awarded.

It follows from *Page* that where a duty of care not to cause physical injury is established, and psychiatric harm results from the defender's negligence, the defender will be liable. In the case of primary victims psychiatric harm need not be reasonably foreseeable. Of course physical harm must be reasonably foreseeable or there would be no duty, but physical harm need not materialise for a claim to be valid. Effectively, where primary victims are concerned, the concept of personal injury has been broadened to include psychiatric harm.

In order to claim as a primary victim the pursuer must be exposed to danger or must reasonably apprehend themselves to be in danger.

SECONDARY VICTIMS

Secondary victims have not been exposed to physical danger themselves. Nevertheless, they have suffered nervous shock, typically as a consequence of witnessing horrific events that have befallen primary victims such as relatives or colleagues. The circumstances in which secondary victims may recover damages in respect of nervous shock are strictly limited and courts take a highly restrictive approach in such cases. In contrast to primary victims, no duty of care to guard against psychiatric harm will arise unless such harm is a reasonably foreseeable consequence of breach.

Reasonable foreseeability of psychiatric harm is a necessary, but not sufficient condition for the existence of a duty of care. In addition, secondary victims have to satisfy three further "proximity" requirements that were established by the House of Lords in the Hillsborough disaster case brought by relatives of the primary victims, *Alcock v Chief Constable of South Yorkshire*. No duty will arise unless: a tie of love and affection is established between the secondary and primary victim; the secondary victim is present at the event or its immediate aftermath; and perception of the event or its immediate aftermath must be direct. Direct perception means that the secondary victim must personally see or hear the event. If the pursuer is told of the incident by a third party the claim will not be met.

The tie of love and affection between primary and secondary victims may be readily presumed in some relationships, for example, between husband and wife or parent and child. However, other relationships are not precluded so in theory recovery should be possible where the primary victim is the same sex partner of the secondary victim or the parties are very close, but not united by any conventional category of relationship. The critical factor is not the type of relationship, but its strength and this is a matter upon which evidence may have to be led. In *Alcock* the first appellant, Robert Alcock lost his brother in law. Another appellant, Brian Harrison lost two brothers. Neither was able to recover in respect of nervous shock in the absence of evidence to show that their relationships with the deceased were particularly close.

Of those appellants whose ties with the primary victims could be presumed, their cases failed because they could not satisfy either or both the other two proximity requirements. Some of the appellants did not arrive at the scene until some eight hours after the event and this was held to be too remote in time to count as presence at the aftermath. The direct perception requirement was not satisfied in some cases where the appellants had learned of the tragedy on TV or heard about it on the radio.

THE STATE OF THE LAW

The view was expressed in *Alcock* that it would not be in every case that all three proximity requirements would require to be satisfied. However, subsequent cases such as *Robertson v Forth Road Bridge Joint Board* in which the pursuer watched his workmate and drinking buddy of twenty years fall to his death, and *McFarlane v EE Caledonia Ltd* in which an oil worker on a supply vessel witnessed at close proximity the series of explosions on the Piper Alpha oil platform, demonstrate the highly restrictive approach taken by the courts where secondary victims are concerned. In neither case did the pursuer succeed. The pursuers were not held to have been involved in the events in a way that would have allowed recovery as primary victims. Their ties with the primary victims were not such as to allow recovery as secondary victims. More recently in *Keen v Tayside Contracts* the pursuer was asked by his supervisor to assist at a particularly gruesome road accident and was refused permission to leave. He was unable to recover in respect of consequent mental harm since he was classed as a secondary victim and had no ties to the victims.

In *Taylorson v Shieldness Produce Ltd* recovery was denied parents who suffered psychiatric illness when their child took three days to die thus demonstrating the persistence of the idea that reparable mental harm must follow some sudden shocking event. On the same basis in *Sion v Hampstead Health Authority*, a father who suffered mental illness having maintained a two-week vigil at the bedside of his dying son was also unable to recover damages. These cases may be contrasted with *Tredget v Bexley Health Authority* in which the birth and death two days later of a child born with serious injuries was treated effectively as a single event.

In *Young v Charles Church (Southern) Ltd* the plaintiff was a scaffolder. When his back was turned a workmate shorted out an overhead power cable with a scaffolding pole. The plaintiff was held by the Court of Appeal to have been within the area of physical danger and recovered damages as a primary victim. However, the point has been made that his nervous shock appears to have been attributable more to witnessing the horrific accident that befell his mate rather than out of fear for personal safety. Considered in the light of *Robertson, McFarlane* and the subsequent case of *Hunter v British Coal* Mr Young appears to have been treated by the courts with uncharacteristic generosity.

In the Scottish case of *Campbell v North Lanarkshire County Council* the pursuer witnessed the horrific aftermath of a series of electrical explosions. The nature of their injuries rendered the appearance of the victims, with whom the pursuer had been working, particularly ghastly. The pursuer returned to the site of the explosion to assist the victims. The pleadings in court focussed upon whether or not the pursuer was a primary victim. Although he had left the scene shortly before the accident, when he returned the event was still continuing. On the basis of his pleadings he appears to have had reasonable grounds to believe himself in danger. Lord Reed allowed a proof before answer, taking the view that the case could not be determined upon pleadings alone. Before reaching a decision it was held necessary to hear evidence on both sides regarding the risks to which the pursuer was exposed.

It is probably fair to say that the current state of the law is regarded as satisfactory by nobody. In England in 1998 the Law Commission argued for reform (Law Com No.249). The Scottish Law Commission has more recently called for radical reform (Scot Law Com No.196). The draft Reparation for Mental Harm (Scotland) Bill appended to the report provides *inter alia* for the abolition of common law rules applying only to mental harm. It is proposed to wipe the slate clean and put liability for mental harm on a statutory basis.

5. VICARIOUS LIABILITY

INTRODUCTION

Vicarious liability concerns the liability of one party for the delictual acts or omissions of another. It can be explained as a modification to the general rule, *culpa tenet suos auctores* (fault binds its authors). Two other maxims are commonly used to justify this modification, *qui facit per alium facit per se* (where one does a thing through the instrumentality of another, he is held as having done it himself) and *respondeat superior* (let the master answer).

In short, while it is normally the case that parties will only be liable for their own conduct, vicarious liability may arise where a delict is committed by a person acting on another's behalf. Where a servant (employee) commits a delict the master (employer) can be called upon to answer for it.

Vicarious liability operates in employment, in agency and in partnership. In all these situations there are relationships in which one party acts on behalf of another. So the employer may be vicariously liable for the acts of employees, the principal for the acts of agents and the other partners for the acts of a single partner. Most of the case law concerns the employer/employee relationship, but similar considerations apply to the other relationships. In agency, for example, the criterion for vicarious liability is whether the agent has acted within the scope of their authority. On vicarious liability for acts of an agent, see for example, *Launchbury v Morgans*. On the vicarious liability of partners see *Dubai Aluminium Co Ltd v Salaam*.

It has been argued that vicarious liability is not so much a matter of legal principle as policy. Where an employer conducts an enterprise that creates risks for others, it is fair that the employer should pay for the consequences of the risks when they materialise. The employer does, after all, take the benefits of the enterprise. The fact that the enterprise is conducted through the instrumentality of others (employees do the work) does not absolve the employer from meeting whatever liabilities arise from the conduct of the enterprise. Moreover, vicarious liability operates as a prompt to employers to promote safe conduct and practices in carrying out the enterprise.

The practical effect of vicarious liability is to give the victim a defender worth suing. Imagine you suffer extensive injuries caused by the negligent driving of a fork lift truck in your local do-it-yourself store. The delinquent truck driver is on a relatively low wage and has no financial assets to speak of. They could not hope to compensate you for your losses. On the other hand the employer, a corporation with substantial assets and a turnover of many millions, is in a position easily to meet your claims. Moreover, the employer will probably have insurance that covers such losses. Where the victim also is an employee, insurance is compulsory under the Employer's Liability (Compulsory Insurance) Act 1969.

It is important to note that vicarious liability arises not only from negligence, but also from intentional wrongdoing. For example, in *Morris v CW Martin & Sons Ltd* an employee committed the tort of conversion by stealing a mink stole deposited with the defendants for cleaning. The employers were vicariously liable to the plaintiff for her loss. In *Photo Production Ltd v Securicor Transport Ltd* an employee deliberately started a fire that burned down the factory he was supposed to be guarding. It was held that vicarious liability arose. Vicarious liability may also arise in respect of fraud. *Taylor v Glasgow District Council* demonstrates that in order for vicarious liability to arise it is not necessary to show that the employer gained any benefit thereby.

Where one party is held vicariously liable the delinquent is not released from liability. Vicarious liability is imposed in addition to the liability of the party at fault. Liability is joint and several. The pursuer may elect to sue either or both parties. In theory the vicariously liable party may recover damages paid to the pursuer from the party at fault as occurred in *Lister v Romford Ice*. In practice this seldom happens.

It should be noted that even where vicarious liability is not established, a case against the defender may be maintained if it can be established that the defender was personally liable to the pursuer. It is not unusual to see a plea of vicarious liability advanced as an alternative to an averment of personal liability. An example would be where a person is injured on trade premises by a falling slate dropped by an employee who is fixing the roof. The employer might be vicariously liable for the negligence of the employee, but could also be personally liable as occupier for harm done due to the state of the building under the Occupiers' Liability (Scotland) Act 1960.

It is not in every case that employers will be held vicariously liable. If you step on a landmine, laid as an illegal remedy against dog fouling in my front garden, there will be no point in seeking reparation from my employer. The delict in this example bears no relation to my employment. Of course there are many situations where the issue of vicarious liability is not so clear cut as in this example. For vicarious liability to arise, the delict must be sufficiently connected to the delinquent's employment. The basic features involved in determining whether conduct gives rise to vicarious liability will be considered below.

The other difficulty found in vicarious liability is in determining for whom the employer is liable. In general employers are vicariously liable for employees, i.e. those under a contract of service *locatio operarum* and not for independent contractors, those under a contract for services *locatio operis faciendi*. However, allocating particular relationships to either category is not always as straightforward as might be thought. This distinction is also considered below.

EMPLOYEE ACTING WITHIN THE SCOPE OF EMPLOYMENT

A good starting point for a Scots text is a dictum of Lord President Clyde in *Kirby v NCB*. An English text would start with *Salmond on Torts*, the source from which Lord Clyde derived his formulation:

> "In the decisions four different types of situation have been envisaged as guides to the solution of this problem. [1] In the first place, if the master actually authorised the particular act, he is clearly liable for it. [2] Secondly, where the workman does some work which he is appointed to do, but does it in a way which his master has not authorised and would not have authorised had he known of it, the master is nevertheless still responsible for the servant's act is still within the scope of his employment. [3] On the other hand in the third place, if the servant is employed only to do a particular work or a particular class of work, and he does something outside the scope of that work, the master is not responsible for any mischief the servant may do to a third party. [4] Lastly, if the servant uses his master's time or his master's tools for his own purposes, the master is not responsible."

Categories [1] and [4] are relatively clear. The difficulties that arise in practice concern the distinction between [2] and [3]. An unauthorised mode of doing an authorised act [2] gives rise to vicarious liability, but an act that is outwith the scope of employment, *i.e.* completely independent of the employer's business [3] does not. However, independent acts may give rise to vicarious liability if they are sufficiently connected with the employer's business. This is considered further below under "recent developments".

In *Kirby* the pursuer was a mine employee who had gone to a part of the pit away from his working place for a smoke. The defender, the employer, was not liable for the injuries sustained in an explosion when a match was lit by an unidentified miner. Going for a smoke was not in any way connected with the pursuer's work, it was done purely for his own purposes and pleasure and, incidentally, was in breach of statute. The pursuer had acted outwith the scope of his employment.

Still on the subject of smoking, the difference between [2] and [3] may be illustrated by contrasting *Kirby* with *Century Insurance Co Ltd v Northern Ireland Road Transport Board*. In an act of monumental stupidity the driver of a fuel tanker lit a cigarette and discarded a match while draining 300 gallons of petrol from his tanker into a garage storage tank. The resulting explosion damaged the garage owner's car and several houses. In this case the driver was acting within the scope of his employment and his employers were therefore vicariously liable. Lighting the cigarette was an unauthorised act, but done while the driver was doing his job. As Lord Chancellor Viscount Simon observed: "They also serve who stand and wait". It was the driver's duty to watch over the delivery. He was negligent in the discharge of his duty, but he was actively discharging his duty while negligent, therefore he was acting within the scope of his employment. *Century Insurance* falls within [2].

The reason *Kirby* was unsuccessful in his claim was that he was "off on a frolic of his own", rather than acting within the scope of his employment. Similarly, in *McLean v Remploy Ltd* the pursuer was the victim of a practical joke, played on him by other, unidentified employees who had tied a length of yarn across a corridor. The Lord Ordinary (Cameron) held that employers could not be held vicariously liable for such frolics. However, such cases turn on their own circumstances and in *Harrison v Michelin Tyre Co Ltd* the defender was found vicariously liable when an employee was injured by a prank. The critical feature has been whether or not the act can be deemed to be within the scope of employment.

The courts have demonstrated a clear tendency to find vicarious liability so long as the employer's purposes are being pursued when the delict is committed. This is so even though the employer's rules have been broken. In *Rose v Plenty* a milkman hired a thirteen year old boy to assist with deliveries in flagrant breach of dairy policy. The boy was injured when the milkman drove the float negligently. The dairy was found vicariously liable since the boy's presence on the float was in pursuance of the employer's business.

The following three examples concern drivers who deviated from their most direct routes in the course of carrying out their employers' instructions. In all these cases employers were found vicariously liable on the basis that the delinquent employees were conducting authorised work in an unauthorised way. Each case demonstrates in successive fashion the extent to which courts will go in order to hold that acts are within the scope of employment and therefore employers are liable. In *Angus v Glasgow Corporation* a lorry driver took a short deviation from his route in order to collect his spectacles from home. He collided with a car. The car driver sued the lorry driver's employers in negligence. In *McLeod v South of Scotland Electricity Board* a van struck and damaged a footbridge that the pursuers were constructing. The driver had been authorised to take the vehicle home, but when a few hundred yards from home he had gone out of his way to drop off a fellow employee and had then taken a further diversion to visit his mother in law. The Lord Ordinary (Wylie) held that the original authorised purpose of the journey had not been wholly superseded.

The final case, *Williams v Hemphill* which went all the way to the House of Lords, shows the most outrageous deviation. A driver was employed to take a boys' brigade company from Benderloch in Knapdale home to Glasgow. Some of the boys prevailed upon the driver to go to Dollar in Clackmannanshire. This was in order to see once again a party of girl guides whom the boys had helped with luggage at Connel station. Instead of turning down the A82 at Crianlarich which would have taken them down Loch Lomondside and into Glasgow by Dumbarton the driver headed by the A85 and A84 for Stirling from where he took an eccentric route for Dollar by the south bank of the Forth and Kincardine. This deviation took the party directly away from Glasgow. Through negligent driving the lorry was overturned on a corner heading into Dollar and there were injuries and fatalities. At all stages of the litigation it was held that the employer was vicariously liable. The dominant purpose of the journey was transportation of the boys to Glasgow, the driver was still engaged in this purpose and the deviation by Dollar was not an independent journey.

RECENT DEVELOPMENTS

The three driver cases and *Rose v Plenty* demonstrate that a broad view is taken of whether conduct is within the scope of employment. Nevertheless, problems have emerged with the old approach that seeks to distinguish between unauthorised modes of doing work and independent acts. A new approach to determining vicarious liability has been pioneered in the Canadian Supreme Court and accepted and applied by the House of Lords in the English case of *Lister v Hesley Hall Ltd*. The new approach is very much a development on the old rather than a departure. It has not met with universal approval and it has been argued that its application should be restricted to cases of intentional harm which is the context from which it emerged. Nevertheless it has been influential in a number of subsequent cases, both Scots and English.

The House of Lords in *Lister* approached vicarious liability as a matter of policy rather than principle and considered that the issue really was whether in the circumstances, it would be fair and just to impose on the employer liability for the conduct complained of. On the *Lister* model the question whether circumstances give rise to vicarious liability will depend on the outcome of the close connection test. Under this test it must be determined whether an act is *sufficiently connected* to employment for it to be fair and just to hold the employer vicariously liable.

The application of this test can be explored through the case law in which the new approach was developed. In *Bazley v Curry* an employee in a residential care home sexually abused one of the children in his care.

The acts were sufficiently connected with his employment for the employers to be held vicariously liable. By contrast in *Jacobi v Griffiths* an employee at a childrens' recreational club sexually abused a brother and sister who attended the club. With the exception of one incident, the abuse took place at the defendant's home. The fact that the defendant had met the children at the club did not establish a sufficiently close connection between the acts and employment. The employers were held by a majority of the Canadian Supreme Court not to be vicariously liable. In *Lister v Hesley Hall Ltd* the warden of a school boarding house sexually abused children in his care in a systematic fashion. There was sufficient connection between the acts and employment for the employers to be held vicariously liable.

The logic of these decisions is clear, but the results are not necessarily those that would be reached under the old approach. This may be demonstrated by reference to *Trotman v North Yorkshire County Council*. The deputy headmaster of a special school was charged with responsibility for caring for a disabled teenager on a foreign holiday. The teacher sexually abused the boy. In seeking to distinguish between unauthorised modes of work and independent acts the Court of Appeal found the employers were not vicariously liable. This was not a wrong decision in a legal sense though it produced an unjust result. Far from being an unauthorised mode of carrying out a duty the acts were held to be a negation of the duty and thus independent. The *Lister* approach, which takes into account the nature and purpose of the act along with the context and circumstances in which it occurred, should avoid such decisions in the future. The broad approach to vicarious liability demonstrated in *Rose v Plenty* and *Williams v Hemphill* is maintained, but now the courts will concentrate on sufficient connection between acts and employment and the old distinction between unauthorised modes and independent acts is arguably redundant. *Trotman* was overruled by the House of Lords in *Lister*.

It can be predicted that where a person charged with the care of children in residence uses their position to commit acts of sexual abuse within the home the employer will be liable. On the other hand if a schoolteacher abuses school pupils in his own home the fact that he has met the children at his work may not establish a sufficient connection between the acts and employment to render the employers vicariously liable. However, a case of this nature is a marginal example. If a relationship of trust and intimacy was developed in the classroom courts might well hold a sufficient connection. The result will depend on all the circumstances of the case. Where an employee uses their position working alongside another to conduct a campaign of sexual harassment, for example, where two persons work in close proximity and one continually contrives to brush up against the other, there is little doubt that the employer will be vicariously liable. However, a party may conduct a campaign of harassment against a fellow employee without sufficient connection between employment and the acts for vicarious liability to arise as was the case in *Ward v Scotrail Railways Ltd*, approved by the House of Lords in *Lister*.

Since the peculiar circumstances of each case play a critical role in determining sufficient connection, it is difficult to make general predictions on the likely outcomes of potential cases.

As a final point vicarious liability for acts of racial abuse may be briefly considered.

The Race Relations Act 1976 s.32(1) states:

> "Anything done by a person in the course of his employment shall be treated for the purposes of this Act (except as regards offences thereunder) as done by his employer as well as him, whether or not it was done with the employer's knowledge or approval..."

In *Jones v Tower Boot Co Ltd* Raymondo Jones sought damages in respect of racial abuse carried out by two fellow employees the Industrial Tribunal held the employer vicariously liable by virtue of s.32. This decision was reversed by the Employment Appeal Tribunal on the basis that the abusers could not be described as acting in the course of their employment. Racial abuse was not an unauthorised mode of working, it was a series of independent acts. The House of Lords, in seeking to give effect to the intention of Parliament, to eliminate racial discrimination, held the employer liable. The words "in the course of his employment", were to be given their ordinary everyday meaning and not construed in accordance with common law rules on vicarious liability. Accordingly, where an employee is subjected to racial abuse by fellow employees, the employer will be vicariously liable under statute and the common law does not apply.

FOR WHOM IS THE EMPLOYER LIABLE?

Vicarious liability is dependent upon the relationship between the delinquent and the liable party. Employers are liable for the delicts of employees, but not for those of independent contractors. In many instances the distinction between employees and contractors is easily made. In employment the parties are linked by a contract of employment which is either permanent or for a fixed term. The contract terminates at the expiry of the term or following the period of notice according to the contract terms. Equally, the employee may be dismissed. This is a contract of service (*locatio operarum*). A contractor on the other hand is on a contract to perform some specific task or service. The contract terminates when the obligations have been discharged, normally when the work has been completed or the service rendered and payment has been made. This is a contract for services (*locatio operis faciendi*).

The difference may be illustrated by comparing a taxi driver, whom one employs in order to get from A to B on a one-off basis, with a chauffeur, employed to drive one's Bentley wherever and whenever one wishes to go. The former is a contractor. The latter is an employee.

Problems arise where the nature of the contract between the delinquent and the employer is unclear or ambiguous. One test that has been used to determine the distinction between employees and contractors concerns the element of control. According to the control test, where the employer can tell the other party not only what to do, but also how to do it the relationship is one of employment. While this approach works well in respect of unskilled work it is less useful where work is skilled or specialised. For example, when the server is down in the Law Department it is the job of the network supervisor to get it running again, but neither the Head of Department, the Dean nor the Principal himself can tell the supervisor how to do it. Nevertheless the supervisor is an employee.

There is a wide range of factors that can be taken into account in determining the nature of the relationship. The element of control may be a factor depending on circumstances. Other factors include: the extent to which the person is integrated into the organisation as a whole; whether the party runs a commercial risk; the intention of the parties; whether payment is in the form of regular wages or salary or for "the job"; whether employers' national insurance contributions are made; whether tax is deducted as PAYE or the party makes their own tax arrangements; pension arrangements; and the way in which the contract may be terminated.

By taking into account multiple factors according to the circumstances rather than adhering to a rigid test the courts are able to produce just results in a multiplicity of differing contractual arrangements. So, for example, in *Short v J&W Henderson Ltd* a docker was held to be an employee of the defending company despite working arrangements very different from that which we would naturally think of as employment.

The defenders were responsible for shipping and unloading a cargo of cement at Campeltown harbour. Dockers at Campeltown were organised so that, whenever a ship was due in, a sufficient number of dockers to unload the cargo was allocated on a strict rota basis. The allocation was made by the local trade union secretary, himself a docker who took part on the rota in turn. There was no foreman or any docker in charge. The shippers paid a lump sum for the discharge of the cargo to a broker who in turn paid that sum to whichever docker had been sent to receive payment. The dockers involved on each occasion then divided the money equally between themselves. The broker stamped the National Health and Unemployment Insurance card of any docker employed for the first time that week, seeking the employers' contribution from the shippers. When three dockers were injured in an accident, it was held in the House of Lords that each docker was under an individual contract of employment with the shipper. A number of factors were deemed relevant and the requirement of control was held satisfied by the fact that the brokers, as agents of the employers, had regularly attended the unloading.

This pointed to supervision. While there had never been any need to dismiss or suspend a docker it was found that had such a need occurred this power would have been exercised by the broker on the shipper's behalf.

In one further example, *United Wholesale Grocers Ltd v Sher*, warehouse owners contracted with the defender for joinery work. Sher entrusted the job to three workmen who were paid daily without any deductions for tax or national insurance. Allegedly, one of the workmen negligently discarded a cigarette that caused a fire in the warehouse. The pursuers sought to hold Sher vicariously liable. In the Outer House Lord Cullen had to determine whether the workmen were employees or independent contractors. While the control exercised by Sher over the way in which the work was done was an important factor, it was not conclusive. This was particularly so since supervision of the men was not necessary in the circumstances. The status of the workmen depended on assessment of all relevant factors. Sher supplied the materials, but the workmen supplied their own tools. It fell to be considered whether the work carried out should be regarded as part and parcel of a business carried out by Sher, or as part of what the men were doing on their own account. Lord Cullen came to the conclusion that they were employees of Sher carrying out work on the warehouse that Sher had contracted to undertake.

In general, employers cannot be held vicariously liable for the delicts of independent contractors although they may become personally liable to their own employees if an incompetent contractor is appointed in breach of the employer's duty to take reasonable care for the safety of employees.

There is one exceptional case, *Marshall v William Sharp & Sons Ltd* in which an employee's widow was able to recover from his employer for the delict of an independent contractor, despite a finding that there was no element of personal liability. The pursuer's husband was a quarry manager who died while checking an electrode spark in a burner. The contractor was an electrician who fired both ignition and fuel buttons on the burner when testing it. The electrician was the only one employed at the quarry and he was perpetually available to the quarry. Working at the quarry took up most of his time. Nevertheless, the Inner House determined that the electrician was an independent contractor, but the defenders were vicariously liable for his act. This case is regarded as controversial although it has been argued that the decision can be supported on grounds of the degree of control exercised by the defenders over the electrician.

PRO HAC VICE EMPLOYMENT

Finally, the situation sometimes arises when courts have to determine which of two different employers is vicariously liable for the delict of an employee. This arises where an employee is lent out or hired. In general, liability rests with the employer with whom the employee has a contract of employment. However, if pro hace vice employment is established this means that the borrower may become vicariously liable. The employer who borrows the person will only become vicariously liable if it can be established that full control over not only what the employee does, but how the employee does it, has passed to the borrowing employer. *Sime v Sutcliffe Catering (Scotland) Ltd* is an example where pro hac vice employment was established. The pursuer's employers were vicariously liable to her in respect of the negligence of outside caterers contracted to operate in her place of work.

Pro hac vice employment is not determined by any contractual agreement between the two employers. Thus, even though a contract provides that the party is to be regarded as a servant of the borrowing employer, this cannot be relied upon in an issue with a third party who was not a party to the contract. In the House of Lords case of *Mersey Docks and Harbour Board v Coggins & Griffith (Liverpool) Ltd* the defendants, a firm of stevedores, borrowed a crane and driver from the Harbour Board. It was held that while the stevedores told the crane driver what to do, the way in which he did it was a matter within his own discretion. This discretion had been delegated to him by the Harbour Board. When the crane driver negligently injured an employee of Coggins & Griffith, the Harbour Board were held vicariously liable.

6. DEFAMATION

INTRODUCTION

People are entitled to conduct their daily lives without having their characters besmirched or their reputation dragged through the mud. They have a legitimate and legally protected interest in what Stair described as: fame, reputation and honour (Institute 1, ix, 4). A person's interest in their reputation is a reparable interest. Accordingly, where that interest is harmed, damages may be sought. Equally interdict may be sought in order to prevent an injurious publication or broadcast from taking place.

The interest in honour and reputation is protected primarily by the law of defamation. There is a related action of verbal injury that is similar, but not identical. Indeed, in some circumstances the law of negligence may provide a remedy.

In modern society personal honour is perhaps less important to most of us than it would have been in the Victorian and Edwardian periods. Norrie (*Defamation and Related Actions in Scots Law,* 1995) has calculated that in terms of numbers, defamation actions reached a peak in the twenty years between 1890 and 1910. Since then cases have become relatively rare. The prime reasons given by Norrie for the relative infrequency of defamation cases are: the demise of the late Victorian idea of honour; the lack of legal aid for defamation actions; the fact that almost no use was made of civil juries in Scotland during the twentieth century; and the modest level of damages awarded in the Scottish courts. Doubtless the last two points are related. The very high levels of damages sometimes set in England by juries are not found this side of the border where civil juries are relatively seldom used.

In English law a distinction is drawn between slander and libel. Broadly, slander may be described as defamation in a transitory form such as speech. Libel may be described as defamation in a permanent form, such as writing. Libel is a criminal offence as well as an actionable tort. Slander gives rise only to civil liability on proof of actual damage. In practice this distinction presents English law with considerable difficulty. No such distinction is drawn in the Scots law of defamation. Defamation in modern Scots law is purely civil although historically there were criminal elements.

ESTABLISHING DEFAMATION

In a nutshell there are three fundamental elements of defamation. The statement must be defamatory, it must be false and there must be malice. It has been said that there must be loss, but personal affront is sufficient to amount to loss, there need be no patrimonial or economic loss. The only further requirement is that the statement must have been communicated. In England, to be actionable, a statement must be communicated to a third party. In Scotland the requirement for communication can be satisfied by communication to the pursuer (*Ramsay v Maclay*). The Scots approach to the rule on communication reflects the availability of solatium for affront or injury to feelings and the fact that there need be no patrimonial loss.

Defamatory capacity

Because malice and falsity are presumed, the focus of the pursuer's effort is likely to be on establishing the defamatory capacity of the statement complained of and the fact that they have been defamed. Whether a statement has the capacity to defame is a question of law. Whether the statement has actually defamed the pursuer is a question of fact.

Whether words have a defamatory capacity may be determined by the application of a test laid down by Lord Atkin in *Sim v Stretch*: "Would the words tend to lower the plaintiff in the estimation of right-thinking members of society generally?"

The test is thus objective. The issue is not what the pursuer understands the words to mean, neither is it relevant to consider what the defender meant by the words. Whether a statement is defamatory is determined by the views of "right-thinking" people. Of course, the court determines what "right-thinking" people think. "Right-thinking" people are reasonable persons who do not hold prejudices.

This brings us to the issue of innuendo. That is the way in which a meaning may be attributed to words that is not present on the face of the statement. For example, the statement that X is a thief is *prima facie* defamatory. The statement that X holds a surprising quantity of electrical goods in a lock up garage is not. However, depending on the circumstances in which the statement is made it may bear the innuendo that either X is a thief or X deals in stolen goods. The onus lies on the pursuer to establish that the statement complained of bears the innuendo contended for.

The question that must be asked is, as Lord Anderson put it in *Duncan v Scottish Newspapers Ltd*:

> "[W]ould a reasonable man, reading the publication complained of, discover in it matter defamatory of the pursuer? Or, put otherwise, the question is, What meaning would the ordinary reader of the newspaper put upon the paragraph which the pursuer complained of?"

There is also a subjective element in the test for defamation. In determining defamatory capacity courts must take into account the type of person likely to have heard or read the statement, the personal circumstances of the pursuer and all the circumstances in which the statement is made. For example, the statement that the pursuer is a hard-drinking brute with an expansive repertoire of obscene verse who handles balls better than Gavin Hastings might well be defamatory if applied to a choirmaster and published in the Church of Scotland periodical, Life & Work. Whereas the same statement applied to a player and printed in a rugby programme might be both intended and regarded as complimentary. The point is that what may be deeply injurious in one context can be unobjectionable in another. The law takes context into account.

Malice and innocent defamation

While liability in defamation is based on malice, the pursuer is not required to prove malice on the part of the defender. Once the statement complained of is established as defamatory, malice is presumed from the harmful nature of the words used. This presumption is rebutted where the defence of qualified privilege applies and so in such cases malice does have to be shown.

The presumption of malice in defamation is one aspect of the law that might be thought to be unsatisfactory. It offends against the general idea of no liability without fault. This is particularly so since liability attaches not only to the person making the defamatory statement, but also to those who repeat or disseminate the statement. This obviously extends to newspaper editors and to broadcasters, but also includes bookshops, libraries and the operators of web pages. The ability of such persons to verify facts or check for defamatory content may be very limited. Despite the absence of any malicious intent to injure, the innocent disseminator of a defamatory statement may nevertheless be held liable. Where defamation is innocent the law extends a defence to persons who can show that they were not the author, editor or publisher of the offending statement. They must show that reasonable care was taken in relation to publication and further, that they did not know and had no reason to believe their actions caused or contributed to the publication of a defamatory statement (Defamation Act 1996, s.1).

The classic example of innocent defamation is the case of *Hulton v Jones* in which the author of a novel created a fictional character with the unlikely name of Artemus Jones. Unfortunately for the author there was a real Artemus Jones. Doubly unfortunate was the fact that Artemus Jones was a barrister. The defendant was liable notwithstanding the fact that the defamation complained of was entirely innocent.

Falsity

Defamatory statements are presumed to be false. Therefore there is no onus on the pursuer to establish the falsity of what has been said. The defender may lead the defence of *veritas* in which case the onus rests on the defender to prove the truth of the statement. If the statement is true, then no action lies in defamation since a defamatory statement is by definition false. Accordingly, *veritas* is a complete defence.

TYPES OF DEFAMATORY STATEMENT

The types of statement or imputation that have given rise to actions in defamation can be listed thus: criminality; immorality; professional incompetence; financial unsoundness; disease or disability; and aspersions against public character (Norrie, 1995). However it must be noted that there is absolutely no requirement that a defamatory statement must fall under any one of these headings.

Criminality

False imputations of criminal conduct have proven a fertile source of litigation. Nevertheless it is not every imputation of criminal conduct that will give rise to liability in defamation since the test of lowering the pursuer in the estimation of "right-thinking" people must be satisfied. All crimes do not carry the same level of social stigma. Accusations or imputations of murder (*Monson v Tussauds*), theft (*Neville v C&A Modes*), lewd and libidinous practices or shameless indecency will clearly have the effect of reducing the social esteem in which a person is held. In *Gecas v Scottish Television* an action was brought by a party accused of involvement in the liquidation of Jews during the second world war. Such an accusation is defamatory, but this case was successfully defended on grounds of *veritas*. There are other crimes which would fail Lord Atkin's test, so for example, if a person is wrongly accused of a parking violation this would not be defamatory since such an accusation would not have the effect of lowering the accused in the esteem of others. Other crimes fall into a grey area so if the accusation is of driving over the legal limit for alcohol this would be considered defamatory now, but might well not have been so forty, thirty or even twenty years ago. Would people think less of you if they believed you had a speeding conviction? Would the answer to this question differ according to whether you were accused of driving at 85mph on the motorway or at 160 mph in a 30 limit on a Yamaha R1? How would you regard a person whom you believed had been convicted of failure to obtain a TV license?

Immorality
Lord Atkin's "right-thinking" people test is sufficiently flexible to allow for the fact that what tends to lower a person in the estimation of other people changes over time. Nowhere is this clearer than in the context of immorality. The objective element of the test allows for social attitudes changing over time. Thus, while it has been held defamatory to imply pre-marital sexual relations (*Morrison v Ritchie & Co*) or a "lack of womanly delicacy" (*Cuthbert v Linklater*) it is very doubtful if any such implication would now lower the pursuer in social esteem. Similarly, in *Brownlie v Thomson* damages were obtained in respect of the pursuer having been called a "blackguard". Blackguard means scoundrel, an insult which carried weight in 1859 when the case was determined but which has passed out of common usage.

Not only do notions of morality change, but in a modern pluralistic society it becomes increasingly difficult to establish the likely reaction of "right-thinking" people since general agreement on some aspects of morality is conspicuously lacking. For example, in certain sections of society it would be deeply insulting and defamatory to suggest that a man is uncircumcised. Nevertheless this sort of consideration can be taken into account by the law through the subjective element of the test for defamation.

Accordingly, precedents for a particular imputation being held defamatory are an incomplete guide to whether similar statements are actionable today or in the future. Actions founded on imputations of immorality were relatively uncommon during the twentieth century in comparison with the nineteenth. Nevertheless imputations on a person's moral character may continue to found actions, the success of which will depend on how the aspersion is viewed by "right-thinking" people and of course, on the context. "Right-thinking" people would probably not shun an individual purely on grounds of homosexuality. Such an accusation was held not defamatory in *Quilty v Windsor*. Equally it can no longer be defamatory to suggest that a couple are cohabiting without being married.

Persons might well lower their esteem of someone believed to be conducting an adulterous relationship, or working as a prostitute. In *Finburgh v Moss's Empires Ltd* the manager of a theatre asked a married couple to leave, calling the wife a "notorious prostitute". One can imagine the degree of personal affront this must have caused. The wife succeeded in recovering damages, the husband did not. The court in 1908 did not find the suggestion that a man kept company with a prostitute defamatory.

Professional competence and professional misconduct

These types of defamatory statement do continue to give rise to litigation. Imputations against a person's conduct in a professional context are likely to have economic as well as social implications. Moreover, professionals may be members of professional bodies willing to fund litigation. There are many examples of cases involving imputations of professional incompetence in the case law ranging from a doctor accused of "gross negligence" (*Simmers v Morton*) to a market gardener accused of letting weeds over-run his plots (*Cadzow v District Commissioners of Edinburgh*). Professional misconduct is slightly different since there need be no suggestion of incompetence. In such instances defamation consists of an allegation which is damaging because of the pursuer's professional position. For example, to accuse a person of being a racist might or might not be defamatory depending on the context. If an allegation is made that a police officer was motivated by racism to arrest a person then that is defamatory following *Fraser v Mirza*.

Financial unsoundness

Allegations of financial unsoundness may offer no comment on the moral character or social acceptability of a person. However, any such aspersion may have severe detrimental economic consequences. The victim may no longer be able to obtain credit, credit already extended may be withdrawn. Allegations of this type are actionable as defamation although there is some difficulty in reconciling this with the test which requires lowering in social esteem. It has been suggested that defamation operates to protect a person's commercial character as well as their private persona.

Disease or disability

In the past the view has been taken that an imputation of insanity or "loathsome disease" or even male impotence is actionable as defamation. However this view does not accord with the view that what is defamatory is that which tends to lower the person in the esteem of right thinking people. Right thinking people are doubtless sympathetic to the ill. Indeed, the twentieth century yielded no cases raised on such a basis. An allegation of illness, whether mental or physical, ought not to be regarded as defamatory. On the other hand an allegation that a person suffers from a sexually transmitted disease might be innuendoed as an allegation of sexual profligacy which might indeed be defamatory.

Aspersions against public character

Politicians and persons in public office in general must bear a great deal of criticism and even abuse. Such elements are part and parcel of public life and a great deal of latitude is accorded those who seek to criticise. After all, the public has a legitimate interest in the criticism of public office bearers whom they either elect directly or who are appointed by elected persons or bodies. Depending on the circumstances in which criticism is made, comments may attract qualified privilege in which case the presumption of malice does not operate. However a distinction has to be drawn between attacks on public and private character. It may not be defamatory to criticise the way in which a council leader does their job, but it is defamatory to suggest that they are corrupt or enervated by base motives. In short the latitude given to criticism of the council leader *qua* public officer is not extended to criticism of the council leader *qua* individual.

It may be noted that the Representation of the People Act 1983, s.106(1) makes it a criminal offence to make a false statement about the personal character or conduct of a candidate for Parliament before or during an election. Any such charge may be defended if it can be shown that there were reasonable grounds for belief in the statement and that the accused did in fact believe it to be true. However, under election conditions the offended politician must reflect on whether either civil litigation or criminal proceedings are likely to redound to their advantage.

DEFENCES TO DEFAMATION

Veritas

Since by definition a defamatory statement is untrue, *veritas* (truth) affords a complete defence. The onus is on the defender to prove the truth of the allegation. When applied successfully this defence rebuts the presumption of falsity.

In rixa

Rixa means a quarrel or brawl. Words uttered in the heat of the moment may be defensible on grounds that they were not seriously intended. It follows that this defence is only available in respect of spoken and not written defamation. The classic example of this defence is *Christie v Robertson*. A misunderstanding arose at an auction when two men both thought they had bought the same horse. When one of them led it away a quarrel ensued in which one man said of the other that he "should have been in the hands of the police twenty times in the last five years". The defence succeeded. Similarly, in the colourful case of *Harper v Fernie* the female pursuer got no damages when called a "damned drunken old whore" during a heated altercation with a neighbour.

Vulgar abuse and sarcasm

Statements that are abusive or sarcastic are treated similarly to words uttered *in rixa*, they are not viewed as seriously intended. Thus great scope is allowed satirical television programmes, magazines and cartoons to lampoon public figures without fear of attracting litigation. No action arises from descriptions as a vampire of Michael Howard, leader of the conservative party during the 2005 general election. Reasonable viewers or readers will not regard mockery or abuse as serious allegation. Similarly football referees cannot seek damages in defamation in respect of statements questioning the marital status of their parents or suggesting severe visual impairment.

Fair retort

If an allegation is made against a person that person is entitled to reply. If the reply contains defamatory elements then it may found an action for defamation, but there is no presumption of malice. Therefore the pursuer will have to establish malice on the part of the defender. The fact that a reply has been made is suggestive of a desire to protect reputation and does not infer malice. This may be seen, for example, in *Gray v SSPCA*. In order to count as a fair retort the reply must be kept within the bounds of relevance. In *Blair v Eastwood* the defender overstepped the boundaries of fair retort when he was accused by the pursuer of having fathered her child. He in turn accused the pursuer of having had sex with at least two other men. This was not a fair retort.

Fair Comment

The defence of fair comment arises in the context of comments or reviews on matters in which the public has an interest. As a matter of policy the law allows considerable freedom of expression, for example, when works of art are reviewed or commented upon. The subject of the comment or review might be a book, a play, a painting, a sculpture, music or even a building. These are examples. The defence is not restricted to comment on art or architecture. The defence might apply to comments on a government policy or criticism of a statement by an individual Minister. Equally it might apply to comment on a court judgment. The defence is generally available in all circumstances where there is an element of public interest.

While it is true that the reputation of an author, artist or architect may be damaged by adverse comments this fact must be balanced against the freedom of the critic to give an honest opinion regarding the worth of the subject under review and against the public interest in reading informed criticism. A further point is that the reading public may make their own judgement on the validity of any comment when presented with the facts upon which the comment is made.

Reviews or comments may be scathing yet, provided certain criteria are met, they will not give rise to liability in defamation. As Lord McLaren stated in *Archer v Ritchie & Co*:

> "The expression of an opinion as to a state of facts truly set forth is not actionable, even when that opinion is couched in vituperative or contumelious language".

In order for the defence to apply three criteria have to be met. First, the statement must be a comment on fact. Secondly the facts must be truly stated. Thirdly the facts must concern some matter of public interest. The onus is on the defender to establish these three criteria. Once these criteria have been established the onus then passes to the pursuer to establish that the comment is not fair. Whether or not a comment is fair is determined by its relevance to the facts.

Thus, for example, provided a book review does not misrepresent the content of the book, the reviewer is at liberty to state that the book is garbage. This is an opinion on a fact (the content of the book) and as such attracts the defence of fair comment. On the other hand if the reviewer states that the author is illiterate and must have slept with the publisher in order to get into print that goes beyond comment on the facts and may indeed be deemed unfair. On reporting a court decision the reporter may set forth the evidence or summarise the case for the prosecution or defence or both and conclude that an acquittal was the wrong result. Despite the fact that such a comment entails imputing criminality to the accused, the defence of fair comment would apply. On the other hand to state that the judge would not recognise a guilty person if he met one in his soup or to accuse the defence of bungling incompetence would go beyond comment on the facts and would render this defence inapplicable.

Privilege

Unlike fair comment the defence of privilege is not generally applicable. The defence of privilege is only available in certain circumstances where the public interest in freedom of speech over-rides any personal interest in reputation.

It is necessary to distinguish between absolute and qualified privilege. Where statements are absolutely privileged they cannot found an action for defamation or verbal injury, even though the statement is motivated by malice or the intent to injure. Where statements are protected by qualified privilege they may give rise to litigation, but the presumption of malice does not operate so the pursuer has the additional burden of proving malice. Malice is difficult to prove and will not be inferred merely from a defamatory statement or imputation. Factors that will assist in establishing malice include the use of particularly harsh or extreme language, prior animosity between the parties or a lack of belief by the defender in the truth of the statement.

Absolute privilege

A successful plea of absolute privilege will render any action in defamation or verbal injury irrelevant. Absolute privilege applies to statements made in the Westminster Parliament whether these are made by MP's or by others, such as witnesses before Select Committees. It also applies to reports and other papers issued under the authority of Parliament including the reports of parliamentary proceedings in Hansard. Absolute privilege applies equally to proceedings before the Scottish Parliament and reports and papers authorised by it by virtue of the Scotland Act 1998, s.41.

Judicial proceedings too attract absolute privilege although here the protection afforded is less than in the case of Parliamentary proceedings. Judges enjoy absolute privilege in the exercise of their judicial function. However this privilege may be lost in the event that a judge makes remarks that are not pertinent to the case before the court. This is in contrast to statements made in Parliament where a defamatory statement that has nothing whatsoever to do with the matter under consideration is nonetheless absolutely privileged. It may be noted that Parliament exercises its own discipline. The absolute privilege enjoyed by judges extends to inferior courts and tribunals as well as to supreme courts.

Similarly advocates and solicitors are protected by absolute privilege, not only in respect of what is said in court, but also in respect of written pleadings. Like judges, this protection may be lost where a defamatory statement is made in circumstances that no reasonable person would view as connected with the matter in hand. Witnesses also enjoy absolute privilege in respect of statements made in evidence and also with regard to statements made to the police or in precognition. See, for example, *Bolam v Burns*. Again, privilege is lost where a witness makes statements that are not pertinent to the case. So long as witnesses confine themselves to answering questions put to them by the judge or by counsel absolute privilege applies. In the event that some extraneous comment is made that has no bearing on the question posed then privilege may be lost.

It should be noted that, in contrast to England, parties to civil litigation in Scotland enjoy only qualified privilege. The parties are present for their own benefit and not in the discharge of any public duty. The possibility of an action in defamation or verbal injury may serve to deter frivolous and vexatious litigation. Of course, if a party is called into the witness box by the opposition, the party is a witness and statements are absolutely privileged. The same does not apply in respect of evidence given by the party on their own behalf.

Members of juries enjoy absolute privilege. While in theory jurors also could lose absolute privilege by some irrelevant remark there is little scope for such an occurrence and there is no case law on this point.

The protection afforded judicial proceedings extends also to quasi-judicial proceedings and tribunals such as public enquiries, employment appeal tribunals and children's hearings.

It may be noted that absolute privilege has been granted by statute to reports and publications of parliamentary ombudsmen. Furthermore absolute privilege attaches to the Lord Advocate in connection with prosecutions on indictment and in turn to procurators fiscal and advocates depute acting in accordance with the Lord Advocate's instructions. Ministers of the Crown are afforded absolute privilege in the proper exercise of their functions.

Qualified Privilege

While the circumstances giving rise to absolute privilege are settled and clear, qualified privilege is relatively fluid in its application. The same statement may attract privilege in one set of circumstances, but not in another. Qualified privilege arises according to the circumstances in which the statement is made rather than being dependent on the status of the person making it or on its nature. Unlike absolute privilege, qualified privilege has no role in verbal injury.

Broadly, qualified privilege arises where a statement is made in response to a duty. Anything defamatory that is communicated may be presumed to be a genuine response to the duty rather than evidence of intent to injure. The requirement that malice be averred and proved follows logically.

The duty need not be legal, but may be social or moral. There are circumstances under which individuals will consider themselves under a duty to speak, for example, in order to report a suspected crime, or in response to a request for a reference for employment or educational purposes.

Where a statement is made in the belief that there was a duty to make it the court will determine whether there was any such duty. The existence of a duty is a question of law. Where there is no such duty the communication will not be privileged. Not only must there be a duty, but the person to whom the communication is made must have a legitimate interest in receiving it.

Consider the following example. I make an allegation to the police that my neighbour is abusing his children. My neighbour sues in defamation. I plead qualified privilege. There is little doubt that I am under a social and moral duty to bring such a concern to the relevant authorities even though, strictly speaking I am under no legal obligation to report crime. The court agrees there is a duty, accordingly my communication is privileged. If my allegation is honestly made my defence succeeds, even though criminal investigation does not find evidence or sufficient evidence to conclude that the children have indeed been abused. If my allegation is malicious then I may well find myself liable in damages. My neighbour may establish malice by proving that I have had insufficient dealings with either himself or his family to form any opinion on whether his children are abused or not. Taken in combination with proof of a long running and acrimonious dispute concerning the height of my leylandii hedge and the fouling of my vegetable patch by his cat he succeeds in proving malice. Had I made the allegation not to the police, but to another neighbour, qualified privilege would not apply. The neighbour would have no legitimate interest in receiving the information.

The press and media in general have a duty to the public to inform. Certain types of reporting are accorded qualified privilege by the Defamation Act 1996, s.15 and Sch.1. Reports of absolutely privileged proceedings, that is, reports of parliamentary and judicial proceedings attract qualified privilege provided the reports are fair and accurate. See, for example, *Cunningham v The Scotsman Publications Ltd.*

The application of qualified privilege to press reports on political matters has been reviewed in the House of Lords in *Reynolds v Times Newspapers Ltd.* Lord Nicholls provided a ten point guide to matters relevant in determining whether such reports would attract privilege. Where privilege is established under these guidelines then a finding of malice is precluded on the authority of the subsequent Court of Appeal case *Loutchansky v Times Newspapers Ltd.* These authorities have since been followed in the Scots case of *Adams v Guardian Newspapers Ltd.*

VERBAL INJURY

The critical differences between defamation and verbal injury may be simply stated. Verbal injury is the appropriate form of action where a reputation has been harmed by words, spoken or written, that are not defamatory. The form of *culpa* that is relevant for liability is malice, but unlike defamation malice is not presumed. Because the statement is not defamatory there is no basis for any such presumption. Therefore malice must be averred and proved. Furthermore a verbal injury is not actionable unless the statement complained of is false. Again, because the statement is not defamatory there is no basis for a presumption of falsity. Accordingly the onus lies on the pursuer to prove that the statement complained of is false.

Verbal injury as distinct from defamation developed out of cases brought by public figures (at least in the local context) such as teachers, ministers and politicians. The basis for complaint was that statements had held them up to public odium, or hatred, contempt and ridicule. The requirements for actionability as outlined in the preceding paragraph were established in 1893 in *Paterson v Welch* and confirmed more recently in *Steele v Scottish Daily Record and Sunday Mail Ltd.* Where it can be shown that a false statement was intended to hold the subject up to hatred, contempt and ridicule damages in the form of solatium are available. Likewise any patrimonial loss is recoverable in damages.

Other forms of verbal injury include slander of title, slander of property and slander of business. Slander of title is a false imputation that a person does not own property that is being sold. An example of slander of property is a statement that a building is in danger of collapsing as in *Bruce v JM Smith*. Such a statement would have the effect of reducing the value or selling price of the property or limiting the market to those interested in the purchase of insecure buildings. Slander of business might be constituted by a statement that a business is incompetently run or is not in a position to meet its liabilities. It can be seen that in none of these situations is the allegation *prima facie* defamatory in the sense of lowering the esteem of the victim in the views of right thinking people, nevertheless considerable harm may be done. The nature of the harm done is most likely to be economic and so, provided it can be shown that the statement is false and that the words were calculated to cause pecuniary loss, damages for patrimonial loss will be available. It will not be necessary to prove actual pecuniary loss by virtue of s.3, Defamation Act 1952. Since the loss is economic rather than affront, communication of the statement to a third party will be required.

NEGLIGENCE

Finally, the law of negligence may be mobilised where harm is caused by words written without care in circumstances where a duty to the pursuer can be established. This occurred in *Spring v Guardian Royal Exchange*. In that case the plaintiff who had been employed by the defendants sought employment with other insurers. The reference provided by the defendants contained false and defamatory statements that effectively scuppered the plaintiff's chances of ever working in insurance again. The action was raised in negligence founding on *Hedley Byrne v Heller & Partners*. The House of Lords treated this as a case of economic loss in which the plaintiff had relied upon the defendants to state facts accurately. It was held by a majority of four to one that there was sufficient proximity between the parties for a duty to arise and there were no policy reasons to deny recovery in damages.

Had the action been raised in defamation the defence of qualified privilege would have applied. References are written in response to a duty and the recipients have a legitimate interest in receiving them. The plaintiff would have been required to prove malice on the part of the defendants and this he could not do. Thus the law of negligence allowed recovery of damages in circumstances where recovery would have been denied under the law of defamation.

7. STATUTORY LIABILITY

INTRODUCTION

The other chapters in this book have been concerned primarily with the common law. In this chapter delictual liability arising from statute is briefly considered.

First, requirements relating to statutory negligence in general are outlined. Two sections follow in which particular forms of statutory liability are considered. These are occupiers' liability and liability for animals.

STATUTORY NEGLIGENCE

A claim in negligence may arise in respect of a duty imposed upon the defender by an Act of Parliament. While in such cases it is clearly not necessary to establish the existence of a duty by reference to the neighbourhood principle, proceeding on the basis of statutory duty casts up its own complications.

Where a statute imposes a duty on a party this does not automatically give the pursuer a right to litigate on the basis of the provision. It must be established that the Act contemplates civil liability in the event of breach. In some Acts, it is expressly stated that breach gives rise to civil liability. The Occupiers' Liability (Scotland) Act 1960, s.1 is an example. In other Acts civil liability is specifically excluded, for example, by the Health and Safety at Work Act 1974, s.47.

Where the Act is silent on whether civil litigation is to be competent the need for construction arises. Taking into account the whole statute, the pre-existing law, the scope and purpose of the statute and for whose benefit the duty was intended, courts seek to determine the intention of Parliament. This process of construction can be seen in the case of *Cutler v Wandsworth Stadium Ltd (in liquidation)*. A bookmaker raised an action for damages against a licensed dog track in respect of their refusal to allow him space on their premises to carry on his trade. He founded on the Betting and Lotteries Act 1934, s.11(2) of which imposed on dog track operators a duty to make space available for bookmakers on the track. It was determined in the House of Lords, upholding the decision in the Court of Appeal, that this provision concerned the regulation of the way in which places of amusement were to be managed. Accordingly the provision was intended to benefit the public at large and not bookmakers in particular. While the duty had been breached, this did not entitle the plaintiff to found on s.11 in a civil action. Where there is doubt regarding whether recourse to civil action is permissible, courts will not allow such action in circumstances where the provision was not clearly intended to benefit the purser. A further example may be found in *Pullar v Window Clean Ltd*.

Where civil action is competent recovery in damages will only be possible where the loss incurred reflects the harm against which Parliament sought to legislate. A very clear example is provided by the case of *Gorris v Scott* in which a statutory duty requiring the shippers of livestock to keep the animals penned in transit was breached. The plaintiff's sheep were swept overboard on voyage. The plaintiff was unable to recover damages since the purpose of the duty was to prevent contagion of disease.

Just as in common law cases it must be shown that the duty was breached and that the loss was caused by the breach. Unlike the common law, in which the standard of care is always the standard of the reasonable man, statute commonly imposes higher standards. Liability may be absolute in the sense that there is no scope for defending a breach, it may be strict in the sense that pursuers are not required to prove fault on the part of defenders. Equally the standard of care may be set at a similar level to the common law. Such is the case in the Occupiers' Liability (Scotland) Act 1960, s.2(1). The standard of care applicable depends on the wording of the statute.

Where a statute imposes absolute liability, evidence of the degree of care taken to avoid the breach will not be relevant in defence. For example, s.22(1) of the Factories Act 1937 provides: "Every hoist or lift shall be of good mechanical construction, sound material and adequate strength, and be properly maintained." In *Millar v Galashiels Gas Co Ltd* a workman was killed through the failure of the brake mechanism on a hoist and an action for damages was brought founding on s.22(1). Every possible step had been taken to ensure the proper working and safety of the mechanism. The failure was unexplained and could not have been anticipated. Nevertheless, the House of Lords found the defenders in breach of a duty and therefore liable in damages.

Part 1 of the Consumer Protection Act 1987 imposes strict liability on producers for property damage or personal injury arising from defective products. Consumers may recover compensation without any need to prove negligence or fault on the part of defenders.

Where claims are pursued on the basis of breach of statutory duty the defence *volenti non fit injuria* is in general inapplicable. Of course, where this defence is expressly provided for in the statute it applies. For example, the Occupiers' Liability (Scotland) Act 1960, s.2(3) provides for the application of *volenti*. The defence of contributory negligence is generally available.

EXERCISE OF DISCRETION BY PUBLIC BODIES

Ministers of the Crown, local authorities and other government agencies exercise powers under statute. The statutory powers such bodies are given commonly involve the exercise of discretion. Where discretion is exercised carelessly to the detriment of an individual, that person can, in principle seek reparation under the common law. In such a case it is necessary to establish that a duty of care was owed to the pursuer in accordance with the normal common law rules of negligence. There has to be foreseeability of harm, proximity must be established and it has to be fair just and reasonable before courts will hold that a duty was owed. However, courts have in the past demonstrated reluctant to recognise duties in such circumstances. So, for example, in *Harris v Evans* a local authority acted on the advice of a health and safety inspector exercising statutory powers in regarding a mobile crane used for bungee jumping. The business was closed down for some time. The pursuers, who had lost profits during this period were unable to establish that a duty of care was owed them by the inspector.

Two types of situation may be identified. First, where a body has discretion on broad policy issues no duty will arise from the way in which that discretion is exercised. So for example, if I suffer food poisoning in a local hotel and attribute this to the fact that the local authority no longer spends sufficient on environmental health, having exercised its discretion to spend more on recreation and amenities instead, this will not be a competent basis for civil action. Even though the hotel has not been subjected to an environmental health inspection, broad policy decisions are not justiciable.

The second type of situation arises where discretion is exercised at an operational level. Principles of administrative law come into play so no liability will arise from the exercise of that discretion unless it is exercised in such an unreasonable fashion that no authority acting reasonably could have exercised discretion in that way. For example, NHS 24 prioritises ambulance calls. If I have called for an ambulance for a relative who is suffering chest pain and the available ambulance is directed first to attend a road traffic accident, no liability will arise even though the relative dies from a heart attack and the victims of the road accident turn out to have no more than superficial wounds. The situation might be different if priority is given a fractured radius and ulna over a clear case of myocardial infarction that has been diagnosed by a doctor at the scene. Such a decision would be so unreasonable that civil liability might well arise.

There is ample scope for courts to decide on policy grounds that a duty of care should be denied. Where administrative decisions have to be made, for example, where social workers and others have to decide whether children should be taken into local authority care, or whether a mental patient is to be released into the community, it may be thought that such decisions are sufficiently difficult without the added factor of taking into account potential litigation. In *X (minors) v Bedfordshire County Council* children sued the local authority in respect of decisions made in care proceedings. Some claimed personal injury as a result of being removed from parental care, others claimed personal injury as a result of not being removed from parental care. It was held that in such circumstances the local authority could not be found liable without proof of fault. This means that an action at common law was viewed as a possibility, but in these circumstances it was not thought fair, just and reasonable to impose a duty of care on social workers.

The enactment of the European Convention on Human Rights into domestic law has prompted developments. Much care has to be exercised by the courts where public bodies appear to be granted wide immunities. Where claims are struck out (in English cases) or held irrelevant (in Scottish) in the early stages of litigation there is a danger that human rights may be breached. The European Convention on Human Rights, Art.6 states, *inter alia*: "In the determination of his civil rights...everyone is entitled to a fair and public hearing within a reasonable time by an independent and impartial tribunal established by law". This concern was first prompted by the decision of the European Court of Human Rights in *Osman v United Kingdom.*

Subsequently in *Z v United Kingdom,* the appeal from *X v Bedfordshire,* it was decided that Article 6 would not be breached simply because a duty of care was denied provided that the litigant had the opportunity to argue that in the circumstances it was fair, just and reasonable to recognise a duty. It was further observed that failure to remove an abused child from parents might amount to a breach of Art.3 which states: "no one shall be subject to torture or to inhuman or degrading treatment or punishment". In *TP & KM v United Kingdom* the European Court of Human Rights observed that a failure to follow fair procedures in child care hearings might amount to a breach of a parent's right "to respect for his private and family life" under Art.8.

As a result of these developments there is a greater readiness on the part of courts to impose duties of care of local authorities. A duty was held owed to a child suspected of being the subject of abuse in *JP v East Berkshire Community NHS Trust.* In *Barrett v Enfield LBC* the House of Lords distinguished *X v Bedfordshire* and found a common law duty of care owed to a child taken into care to provide support mechanisms against potential mental harm.

OCCUPIERS' LIABILITY

Liability for negligence arising from defective premises or dangers on land is governed by the Occupiers' Liability (Scotland) Act 1960. In fact liability under this statute is not restricted to heritable property, but is extended by s.1(3)(a) to include "...any fixed or moveable structure, including any vessel, vehicle or aircraft, and to persons entering thereon." For example, if a passenger in your car dies from carbon monoxide poisoning, because the seal on the exhaust manifold leaks and exhaust gasses enter the passenger compartment the case against you would proceed on the basis of the Act.

The Act imposes a duty on occupiers or those having control. This may be the owner, equally the property may be let and the tenant will be the person in occupation. The landlord will not be the person upon whom the duty is imposed unless they are responsible under the terms of the lease for maintenance or care of the premises (s.3(1)). If the premises are unoccupied then generally the owner will be subject to the duty since the owner has control. Broadly, the duty lies on the party with effective control. Identification of this party is governed by the common law by virtue of s.1(2).

The duty imposed by the Act is set out in s.2(1). "The care which an occupier of premises is required, by reason of his occupation or control of the premises, to show towards a person entering thereon in respect of dangers which are due to the state of the premises or to anything done or omitted to be done on them and for which the occupier is in law responsible shall, except in so far as he is entitled to and does restrict, modify or exclude by agreement his obligations towards that person, be such care as in all the circumstances of the case is reasonable to see that that person will not suffer injury or damage by reason of any such danger."

It must be noted that liability is not strict, the onus is on the pursuer to establish that the defender was at fault.

The next point to note is that the standard of care imposed is that which is reasonable in the circumstances. The standard depends on the circumstances so the occupier is obliged to go to greater lengths to guard against hidden dangers than against obvious ones since the nature of the danger may be taken into account in determining the standard of care applicable. So far as injury caused by obvious dangers is concerned a pursuer may be deemed to have assented to the risk (s.2(3)). So, for example, there is no duty on a landowner to fence a fast flowing burn. A visitor to the land may be deemed to have assented to the risk if she attempts to cross and is drowned. However this point depends on the type of person who may foreseeably enter the land. If it is foreseeable that very young children will enter the land unaccompanied then this alters the circumstances and the standard of care owed them is greater than it would be in respect of adults.

A duty is owed persons who enter the land or premises and it does not matter whether such persons are entitled to be there or not. Accordingly a duty of care is owed to trespassers. However, the duty may be considered discharged if trespassers have to overcome an obvious hurdle to gain access such as a locked door or high fence. A trespasser cannot break into a lockfast building and then sue under the Act if he is then injured when a rotten floor gives way beneath his feet. On the other hand a trespasser who falls into a bear pit, is caught in a gin trap or mutilated by a landmine will have recourse to the law. For examples of cases involving trespassers and discussion on the way in which the standard of care owed is affected by the age of the pursuer see *McGlone v British Railways Board*; *Titchener v British Railways Board*; and *Devlin v Strathclyde Regional Council*.

A further point to note is that the duty imposed by the Act may be modified or excluded by agreement. Where the premises in question are "business premises" any such modification is subject to the Unfair Contact Terms Act 1977, s.16 of which renders any attempt to exclude or limit liability in respect of personal injury or death void. Other terms are subject to a test of reasonableness. Business (and therefore business premises) is widely defined in s.25(1) and covers government bodies, public authorities and professions as well as manufacturers, retailers and service providers. Contracts allowing persons to enter onto land are expressly covered by the Act (s.15(2)(d) and (e)). In order to be effective to exclude or limit occupiers' liability terms have to be very carefully drafted in accordance with common law rules on the construction of exemption clauses.

Finally, the standard of care imposed by the Occupiers' Liability (Scotland) Act does not detract from or relieve the occupier of liability in respect of any other duty imposed on particular premises or types of premises by any other statute or rule of law (s.2(2)).

LIABILITY FOR ANIMALS

The Animals (Scotland) Act 1987 imposes strict liability, that is, liability without any requirement on the pursuer to prove *culpa*, on the keepers of certain animals in certain circumstances. Under the pre-existing common law the keepers of animals *ferae naturae* (of a wild disposition) were presumed to know of the animal's dangerous propensities and were strictly liable for harm resulting from a failure to confine or control the animal. The keepers of animals *mansuetae naturae* (of a gentle disposition) were liable only if it could be proved that either they were aware of the particular animal's dangerous propensities or if they were negligent. The Act supersedes the common law strict liability regime. The old distinction between animals *ferae naturae* and *mansuetae naturae* has become redundant. However, common law actions may still be raised in negligence where harm is caused by animals. The normal rules of negligence apply and the fact that the agent of harm is an animal is largely irrelevant.

Under the Act strict liability attaches to the keeper of the animal as defined in s.5. The keeper is the person who owns the animal or is in possession of it or, where the animal is owned by a child below the age of sixteen, the keeper is the person with actual care and control of the child. The owner remains the keeper of an abandoned animal. Section 3 allows the occupier of land onto which the animal has strayed to detain it. Where this right is exercised the person detaining the animal does not become the keeper.

Strict liability is imposed on the keeper in the event that the animal causes injury or damage (s.1(1)). However not all animals are covered by the Act and not all types of harm or injury caused by those animals give rise to liability under the Act.

Section 1(1)(b) provides that keepers shall be liable if: "the animal belongs to a species whose members generally are by virtue of their physical attributes or habits likely (unless controlled or restrained) to injure severely or kill persons or animals, or damage property to a material extent and (c) the injury or damage complained of is directly referable to such physical attributes or habits.

These provisions operate subject to s.1(4) and (5) so liability under the Act does not arise where either the injury "consists of disease transmitted by means which are unlikely to cause severe injury other than disease" or where injury or damage is caused by "the mere fact that an animal is present on a road or other place."

This means that a farmer will not be strictly liable if foot and mouth disease spreads from his herd to other animals. Liability will arise where rabies is transmitted through a dog bite since a bite may cause severe injury. Where, as sometimes happens, a cow escapes from a field and causes a motorway pile-up the Act will not apply. It would have to be established that the damage caused was attributable to the physical attributes or habits of cows. In situations where liability does not arise under the Act there may be liability at common law, but the pursuer will have to prove negligence or some other form of *culpa*.

Some of the animals covered by the Act are specified. Thus dogs and all animals within the meaning of s.7(4) of the Dangerous Wild Animals Act 1976 are included on the basis that they are deemed likely, in the absence of control or restraint to "injure severely or kill persons or animals by biting or otherwise savaging, attacking or harrying" (s.1(3)(a)). The Schedule of the 1976 Act provides a long list of such animals that includes crocodiles, coral snakes, tigers and wolves. Other animals are listed in the 1987 Act s.1(3)(b) on the basis that they are likely to cause property damage, particularly to crops, when foraging. The animals thus specified are "cattle, horses, asses, mules, hinnies, sheep, pigs, goats and deer". It must be noted that the absence of a particular animal from any of these statutory lists does not exclude that animal from coverage by the Act. Any animal could be included provided it fits within the definition in s.1(1)(b). However, viruses, bacteria, algae, fungi and protozoa are specifically excluded by virtue of s.7. According to accepted biological taxonomy none of these are, in any sense, animals.

Liability imposed by the Act is strict, it is not absolute so there are a number of defences provided for by s.2. No liability arises under the Act if the harm sustained was wholly due to the fault of the victim or the keeper of another animal where that animal is the victim. Furthermore the defence of *volenti non fit injuria* is available in both these circumstances.

As noted under occupiers' liability a duty of care is owed to trespassers. The 1987 Act, s.2(1)(c) provides a defence where a person or animal is injured when trespassing on the keeper's land. In such circumstances, while there may be liability based on fault under the

Occupiers' Liability (Scotland) Act, the keeper is relieved of strict liability under the Animals (Scotland) Act. However, where the animal causing the injury is on the land "wholly or partly for the purposes of protecting persons or property" then the s.2(1)(c) defence is disapplied by s.2(2). Liability will be strict unless the use made of the guard animal was reasonable and if the animal is a guard dog, the use made of the dog must comply with s.1 of the Guard Dogs Act 1975. Compliance with this provision requires guard dogs to be under the control of their handlers or secured so that they cannot roam freely about the premises. Moreover warning notices must be exhibited at every entrance to the premises.

Thus, if I trespass through a field and am gored by a bull, liability will not be strict assuming that the bull has not been placed in the field to act as a guard. I will have to prove negligence or some other form of *culpa* on the part of the defender. If I climb over a garden wall and am mauled by a jaguar, let loose in the garden to act as a guard, then liability will be strict since the use of a jaguar as a guard animal is not reasonable. If I enter a scrapyard and am bitten by a guard dog roaming the premises outwith the control of a handler then liability will be strict. On the other hand if the dog is chained up and there are warning notices at all entrances then I will not recover damages unless I can establish *culpa*.

----

8. NUISANCE

INTRODUCTION

Nuisance emerged as a doctrine of Scots law during the mid-eighteenth century. Nuisance in English law has a much longer history dating back to the twelfth century. There are important differences between the jurisdictions. In Scots law no distinction is drawn between public and private nuisance. Nuisance in Scots law is and always has been relatively narrow in scope, the term has never been applied to the broad range of circumstances described in England as "nuisances". The *plus quam tolerabile* test which is determinant of nuisance in Scots law is unique to this jurisdiction. In Scotland nuisance is always determined on a balance of interests between the parties. This is not the case in England where nuisance may be sub-divided into different forms, in some of which balancing interests is not a relevant means of proceeding (*Hunter v Canary Wharf*).

Finally, Scots law takes a distinctive approach to determining the basis for liability in reparation. Following the House of Lords case of *Strathclyde Regional Council v RHM Bakeries (Scotland) Ltd* liability in reparation in respect of nuisance proceeds on the basis of *culpa*. Prior to *RHM* there had been a lengthy period in which liability was argued to be strict. While this issue was resolved in *RHM* that case did not serve to differentiate nuisance from negligence. As Lord President Hope stated in the First Division in *Kennedy v Glenbelle*:

> "But the analysis of the authorities in that case did not go into the difficult question as to what types of delictual conduct on the part of the defender, amounting to culpa or fault on his part, are actionable on the ground of nuisance and what types are actionable by reference to the ordinary principles of negligence."

Such an analysis was conducted in *Kennedy*. Lord Hope reviewed the concept of *culpa* in the context of liability in reparation generally. It is clear from this analysis that where harm is caused unintentionally "the ordinary principles of negligence will provide an equivalent remedy". The relevant form of *culpa* in nuisance is intention or recklessness. In *Kennedy* an averment of "a deliberate act done in the knowledge that harm would be the likely result" was held relevant to ground a reparation action for nuisance.

This means that nuisance can be seen as a delict of intention albeit it is important to note that intention does not connote the direct intent to injure, but may be inferred from a deliberate act done in the knowledge that harm will almost certainly follow. Negligence, on the other hand operates where there is a mere risk of harm. From the authorities considered by Lord Hope it appears that such knowledge may be constructive. The issue is not what the defender actually knew, but what ought to have been apparent to a reasonable person in the position of the defender.

If nuisance is seen as a delict of intention then this has great advantages for the general coherence of the doctrine. On coherence, one critical point is that nuisance is established on the *plus quam tolerabile* test. This test measures the gravity of the harm. The test is a mechanism whereby the court considers whether the invasion of the pursuer's right to comfortable enjoyment of their property is sufficiently serious to amount in law to nuisance. If the harm is greater than a reasonable proprietor could be expected to tolerate then nuisance is established. If, in addition *culpa* is established then there is liability in reparation for nuisance.

It has been argued strongly by Professor Whitty in the *Stair Memorial Encyclopaedia* (see "*Nuisance*", paras 87 & 89) that the *plus quam tolerabile* test is inapplicable in cases of unintentional harm. This is because in unintentional harm cases potential gravity of harm is taken into account at a different stage, in determining whether or not a duty of care arises. If liability for negligent acts were to be determined on the *plus quam tolerabile* test then, in cases where the harm was material the test would always be positive and there would always be liability, even in circumstances where the risk of material harm was so slight that the defender was entitled to ignore it. This would impose strict liability contrary to the rule in *RHM*. By regarding nuisance as a delict of intention this problem is averted and it is clear that the *plus quam tolerabile* requirement is applicable in every case of nuisance as it was originally intended to be.

Nonetheless, while there are nuisance cases subsequent to *Kennedy* such as *Anderson v White* and *Powrie Castle Properties v Dundee DC* in which *culpa* is averred in terms of "a deliberate act done in the knowledge that harm would be the likely result" there is one case, *The Globe(Aberdeen) Ltd v North of Scotland Water Authority* in which *culpa* was averred in terms that appear much more like negligence and in one further case, *British Waterways Board v Moore & Mulheron Contracts Ltd* the sheriff clearly viewed negligence as a relevant form of *culpa* in an action grounded on nuisance. We can conclude that while there is clear authority to support the view that intention and recklessness are relevant forms of *culpa* in a nuisance action and negligence is not, this point is perhaps not yet fully accepted.

From *RHM* a possible exception arises to the general rule that liability depends on *culpa* where property harm has followed alterations on the course of a natural stream. The relevant authority is the House of Lords case of *Caledonian Railway Co v Greenock Corporation.* This case was long understood to be an authority that supported strict liability for property harm. *Caledonian* was distinguished in *RHM*. The case may best be regarded as misunderstood. The unreported parts of the judgement, particularly the opinion of Lord Dewar in the Outer House make clear that the defenders were at fault. The pursuers succeeded in establishing the negligence of the defenders at first instance. *Caledonian* has only been regarded as involving nuisance in retrospective analysis. The view that *Caledonian* supports a doctrine of strict liability must be highly doubtful.

THE NATURE OF NUISANCE

Nuisance by its nature normally arises between neighbours although it is not the case that properties must be adjoining even though nuisance has at times been described as operating between adjoining proprietors. The essence of nuisance is that the defender is carrying out some activity on their land that interferes with the comfortable enjoyment of the pursuer's property, because the activity causes discomfort or inconvenience. However, it is not a legal requirement that the source of harm is on land owned or occupied by the defender. In *Allison v Stevenson* a lady was interdicted from feeding pigeons in the street. The droppings blocked the pursuers' roans and drainpipes.

Nuisance in Scotland up until the end of the nineteenth century was concerned almost exclusively with what may broadly be termed as pollution. Thus actions were brought in respect of pollution of water and air, in respect of unusual noise, unnatural heat and vibration. Examples include *Dowie v Oliphant* in which the boiling of whale blubber was interdicted and *Johnston v Constable* in which the alleged nuisance was a steam engine operating in a tenement.

It has been argued that there was such a thing as nuisance *contra bonos mores,* meaning that immoral displays could be a form of nuisance, but there is almost no authority to support this category beyond the sole case of *Scott v Cox* in which the hanging to dry of ox hides within sight of a public road was deemed offensive to sight and interdicted as a nuisance. It has also been argued that there was such a thing as a dangerous nuisance although this is problematic. Dangers, when they materialised and harm resulted tended to give rise to reparation actions grounded on negligence rather than nuisance. Prospective and present dangers such as fire hazards could indeed be interdicted in nuisance as occurred in *Vary v Thomson* in which a blacksmith's operation in the vicinity of thatched houses was interdicted. Finally, Bell's description of nuisance includes the obstruction of "the public means of commerce and intercourse, whether in highways or navigable rivers" (*Principles*, para.974). This is very much an undeveloped aspect of nuisance in Scotland and such infringements will usually be dealt with by other means.

Almost all eighteenth and nineteenth century nuisance cases were actions for interdict. People found life in their homes intolerable because, for instance of smoke or noise. Reparation was sought in nuisance in only a handful of cases in which physical harm to property was consequent upon either air or water pollution. In more recent times the relative proportions of interdict to reparation cases has changed. Between 1976 and 2000 there were twice as may actions for reparation reported as those for interdict. Traditional nuisance actions to interdict polluting activities declined as a consequence of Public Health Legislation and Planning regimes so that during the twentieth century such cases became infrequent. Planning meant that polluting processes were less likely to occur in residential areas and Public Health legislation meant that where nuisance did arise it could be dealt with by means other than the common law. Moreover, during the early twentieth century nuisance came to be understood as an infringement of a property right rather than as a state of affairs itself. This allowed for expansion of the scope of nuisance so that material harm to property has come to be understood as nuisance, whether or not it is consequent upon pollution. In practise this expansion in scope has been limited to property harm caused through flooding and deprivation of support for buildings. Nuisance, however need no longer be limited in scope by the way in which the harm is caused. It is thought following *Kennedy v Glenbelle*, that nuisance is the appropriate ground of action wherever property harm amounting to nuisance is caused intentionally.

It is important to note that while *culpa* must be shown in cases where damages are sought this is not the case in actions for interdict. To obtain an interdict it is necessary to establish nuisance, it is not necessary to prove *culpa*.

Nuisance has sometimes been described as a continuing state of affairs rather than an isolated event. In the normal case this is a fair description, indeed interdict will only be awarded in respect of a source of disturbance or harm that is anticipated to either continue or take place in the future. However, it is perfectly clear that damages may be sought in respect of a one off event such as flooding from a burst sewer so while a continuing state of affairs is the normal case in nuisance it is not a requirement for an award of damages.

ESTABLISHING NUISANCE

The right protected by the doctrine of nuisance is the right to comfortable enjoyment of property, free from serious disturbance, substantial inconvenience or material harm. The modern authority on the constitution of nuisance in Scots law is *Watt v Jamieson.*

In order to obtain a remedy against an interference with the right to comfortable enjoyment it is necessary to establish that the invasion amounts to nuisance. This is achieved by application of the *plus quam tolerabile* test. Nuisance is considered from the standpoint of the victim. Taking relevant circumstances into consideration the court must consider whether the interference to which the victim is exposed is *plus quam tolerabile*, that is, more than reasonably tolerable. An action cannot be defended solely on the ground that the defender's activities are reasonable although this is a factor that may be taken into account in balancing the interests of the parties. As Lord President Cooper stated in *Watt*:

> "[I]f any person so uses his property as to occasion serious disturbance or substantial inconvenience to his neighbour or material damage to his neighbour's property, it is in the general case irrelevant to plead merely that he was making a normal and familiar use of his own property. The balance in all such cases has to be held between the freedom of a proprietor to use his property as he pleases and the duty on a proprietor not to inflict material loss or inconvenience on adjoining proprietors and adjoining property; and in every case the answer depends on considerations of fact and degree... The critical question is whether what he was exposed to was *plus quam tolerabile* when due weight has been given to all the surrounding circumstances of the offensive conduct and its effects."

The relevant circumstances that may be taken into consideration in the process of balancing the parties' interests may be summarised as follows. On the pursuer's side it is relevant to consider: the type of harm; the extent of the harm; the social value of the use or enjoyment invaded; the suitability of that use to the locality; the sensitivity to harm of the pursuer or property affected; and the burden on the pursuer of implementing protective measures. On the defender's side it is relevant to consider: the primary purpose of the conduct or operation; the suitability of the operation to the locality; and the practicability of remedial measures.

RELEVANT FACTORS ON THE PURSUER'S SIDE

An invasion of comfortable enjoyment in terms of disturbance or inconvenience is less likely to lead to a reparation claim than actual physical harm. In such cases interdict will normally be the remedy sought. Reparation for personal injury is not excluded where it is incidental to nuisance. An example is the case of *Shanlin v Collins* where a woman suffered mental harm as a result of the barking of a neighbour's dogs. Physical harm may be to plants, crops, shrubs or trees, not just buildings or structures. Equally there may be harm to movable goods as in *Ireland v Smith* in which the contents of a larder were destroyed by dust from a neighbour's chickens. Prospective harm may be interdicted as in *Fleming v Hislop* where the defenders were interdicted against setting light to bings.

The harm must be material. Disturbance must be substantial, inconvenience serious. Even in the case of physical damage it must be shown that the harm is material. There is a difference between the destruction of a field of crops and withered leaves on particularly sensitive shrubs. In determining materiality it is relevant to consider the degree and duration of the invasion. Noise disturbance is not simply a matter of volume, but there may be an element of quality. Thus noise may be more than reasonably tolerable where persons are subjected in their homes to the sound of animals being dispatched in a slaughterhouse, as in *Kelt v Lindsay* whereas louder noises from other sources might not possess the same disturbing qualities. People can reasonably be expected to put up with temporary disturbances such as caused by road works. Equally, time is relevant so bell ringing might be tolerable during the day, but a different matter in the middle of the night. A tourist season such as the Edinburgh Festival may increase the level of disturbance that must be tolerated.

There is not much discussion in the case law on the social value of the use invaded. It is clear however that lawful uses whether residential, industrial, commercial or recreational can be protected.

The relation between the use of land invaded and the character of the locality is less relevant to physical harm than it is to comfortable enjoyment. This does not mean that it is of no relevance and it has been argued that the strict division found between the types of harm in the English case of *St Helens Smelting Co v Tipping* does not apply in Scotland. In *Watt v Jamieson* Lord Cooper considered that locality was generally relevant in nuisance and *Watt* involved physical harm. In *Maguire v Charles McNeil Ltd* the Archbishop of Glasgow among other pursuers failed to interdict the use of drop hammers in a forge. He was resident in a district in which there was much heavy industry. Nevertheless, even in such circumstances it is clear that a material increase in existing disturbance may give rise to a successful action in nuisance.

The sensitivity to harm of the pursuer or the pursuer's property is a relevant consideration in balancing the parties' interests. The *de minimis* rule operates. In nuisance this has been expressed as: *lex non favet delicatorum votis*, the law does not consider the wishes of the fastidious. Particularly sensitive land uses or extraordinarily sensitive persons may not be protected against disturbance that the reasonable occupier would be able to tolerate. However, in the context of personal injury the thin skull rule in *McKillen v Barclay Curle* was followed to allow reparation for nervous debility in *Shanlin v Collins*. In *Armistead v Bowerman* the pursuer failed to obtain damages when fry were destroyed in a fish hatchery as a result of the defender's logging operations. In such sensitive circumstances there is a greater onus on the victim to implement prophylactic measures.

If one can easily protect oneself from disturbance by adopting simple remedial measures such as shutting windows or airing rooms then it is unlikely that there will be a finding of nuisance. On the other hand one is not expected to remain indoors in order to avoid noise or smoke disturbance in the garden. It is not the case that there will be no finding of nuisance where it is simpler and cheaper for the victim to adopt remedial measures than it is for the defender to abate.

RELEVANT FACTORS ON THE DEFENDER'S SIDE

As noted, the reasonableness of the defender's use of land is not a complete defence, but a factor that may be weighed in the balance. Socially useful conduct, such as that which generates employment is more likely to be regarded as reasonable compared with unlawful, malicious or indecent activities. Temporary interferences such as road works must be borne, but duration may prove relevant as in *The Globe v North of Scotland Water Authority*. In this case the pursuers were allowed a proof before answer where road works scheduled to last six weeks continued over nine months. Mud on the pavement from the operation was alleged to have discouraged custom resulting in a reduction in takings in a pub.

The Social utility of an activity cannot override the interest of the victim in their use of land. This is demonstrated in *Ben Nevis Distillery (Fort William) Ltd v The North British Aluminium Co Ltd*. The operation which the pursuers sought to have interdicted involved 72 per cent of UK aluminium production and a significant number of jobs. In this case interdict was awarded, but its operation was suspended to allow the defenders to implement remedial measures. A similar result was achieved in *Webster v Lord Advocate* in which a resident found the noise from preparations for the Edinburgh Tattoo intolerable.

It must be noted that interdicts may be drawn up in a way that allows for the continuation of an activity, but not in such a way as to give rise to nuisance. In this way interdict can be used to regulate activities and effect abatement of nuisance. It must also be noted that while the Court of Session has power to suspend an interdict this power is exercised where either, in the words of Lord McLaren in *Clippens Oil Co v Edinburgh & District Water Trustees*:

> "the granting of immediate interdict would be attended with consequences to the rights of the respondents as injurious, or possibly more so, than the wrong that was complained of or…because the effect of an immediate interdict would be to cause some great and immediate public inconvenience."

Before the power to suspend interdict is exercised it is necessary first to reach a finding on the facts (*Ben Nevis Distillery*).

The less suitable to the character of the locality the more likely an operation is to be held to amount to nuisance. Reference may be made to the Local Development Plan whereby land is zoned for residential, industrial or recreational purposes, but this will not necessarily be conclusive since smoke or noise may travel from an industrial zone to a residential one. The correct application of the planning process does not preclude a finding of nuisance.

Where harm is found to be more than reasonably tolerable evidence of care taken will not preclude a finding of nuisance, however it may go some way to establishing the defender's case. Abatement may be required by the terms of interdict. Equally pronouncement of final interdict may be deferred to allow remedial measures to take place.

DEFENCES

Defences must be distinguished from factors taken into account in the process of applying the *plus quam tolerabile* test. A defence, if established will override a finding of nuisance.

Statutory authority for the operation complained of may provide a defence, but only where nuisance is the inevitable outcome of the operation irrespective of measures that may be taken to effect abatement. The defender may be called upon to show that all care has been taken, but nuisance is the inevitable outcome.

Acquiescence affords a defence equivalent to *volenti non fit injuria* in other areas of delict. *Volenti* does not appear to apply since the rule is that it is no defence that the complainer came to the nuisance. See, for example, *Fleming v Hislop* and *Webster v Lord Advocate*.

For acquiescence to succeed as a defence it is necessary to show that the pursuer had full knowledge of and consented, not merely to the activity complained of, but also to the harm or disturbance. This consent must be shown by something more positive than silence or a failure to object although tolerance of the situation over a long period of time will point towards acquiescence. Acquiescence will not preclude an action where there is a material increase in the level of disturbance or harm.

Contributory fault has no role to play in nuisance. The Law Reform (Contributory Negligence) Act 1945 does not apply. Any role played by the pursuer, for example, a failure to take simple remedial measures may be taken into account in balancing the interests of the parties.

It is not possible to acquire a prescriptive right to create a nuisance. On the other hand the right to object to nuisance may be lost after 20 years under s.8 of the Prescription and Limitation (Scotland) Act 1973. The right to seek reparation will also be lost after 20 years by virtue of s.8. The prescriptive period does not begin to run from the start of the offensive operation, but from the point at which it amounts to nuisance.

STATUTORY NUISANCE

Section 79(1) of the Environmental Protection Act 1990 lists statutory nuisances as follows:

(a)   any premises in such a state as to be prejudicial to health or a nuisance;

(b)   smoke emitted from premises so as to be prejudicial to health or a nuisance;

(c)   fumes or gases emitted from premises so as to be prejudicial to health or a nuisance;

(d)   any dust, steam, smell or other effluvia arising on industrial trade or business premises so as to be prejudicial to health or a nuisance;

(e)   any accumulation or deposit which is prejudicial to health or a nuisance;

(f)   any animal kept in such a place or manner as to be prejudicial to health or a nuisance;

(g)   noise emitted from premises so as to be prejudicial to health or a nuisance;

(ga)   noise that is prejudicial to health or a nuisance and is emitted from or caused by a vehicle, machinery or equipment in a street or in Scotland, road;

(h)   any other matter declared by any enactment to be a statutory nuisance.

Many of the situations that once gave rise to common law nuisance actions are now regulated under this provision. One of the key features of the legislation is that mobilisation of the law is carried out by the Local Authority. The authority is under a duty to detect statutory nuisances and, where complaints are brought, to take reasonable steps to investigate. Where statutory nuisance is found, the authority is obliged under s.80 to issue a notice to ensure that the nuisance is abated. Those on whom the abatement notice is served have a right of appeal to the sheriff court.

Contravention of an abatement notice constitutes a criminal offence (s.80(4)).

Accordingly, if one suffers discomfort or inconvenience from some source regulated by the Environmental Protection Act it is more simple to complain to the local authority than to embark on the process of seeking interdict through the civil courts. However, the aggrieved citizen is not entirely dependent upon the response of the authority. Section 82 allows for direct application to the sheriff court by individuals.

There are a large number of provisions dotted around statute law which deal with nuisance. However, in this brief treatment one final example will suffice. Imagine you live in a tenement flat and your neighbour practises the electric guitar throughout the night at full volume. This could be the subject of interdict. However, the most straightforward way of dealing with the problem is usually to call the police, on the basis that your neighbour is giving reasonable cause for annoyance. If your neighbour fails to desist, having been ordered to do so by a constable in uniform, they will have committed an offence under s.54(1) of the Civil Government (Scotland) Act 1982.

Of course the enforcement of these statutory provisions depend on action by the empowered authorities. The common law may be thought to play an important residual role in circumstances where statutory bodies fail to act.

---

9. NOMINATE DELICTS

INTRODUCTION

The delicts considered in this chapter may be termed nominate delicts, because they have names. Admittedly defamation and nuisance are also nominate delicts, but these merit separate treatment in their own chapters.

There is no definitive and exhaustive list of nominate delicts. One historically important delict, assythment was abolished by statute in 1976. Others, such as seduction have dropped out of practical use. Still others, notably spuilzie have become obscure and difficult. At the same time new delicts continue to emerge. Harassment is a creation of statute albeit the wrong struck at was recognised as such by the common law. In the economic delicts it is a moot point whether there is a multiplicity of delicts or whether a number can be subsumed under the general head of wrongful interference with business.

In one important sense there is no real need for a definitive list of delicts in a jurisdiction in which there is a general principle of recovery in damages for loss wrongfully caused. As Professor Norrie has expressed the point: "The Law of Scotland has never operated within strict and exclusive classes of action".

This chapter considers briefly a selection of the nominate delicts.

DELICTS AGAINST THE PERSON

Assault

Assault is both a crime and a civil wrong. Where the perpetrator has been convicted in the criminal courts a compensation order in favour of the victim may be made in terms of the Criminal Injuries Compensation scheme. Occasionally, where prosecution is not successful a civil action may be pursued. Even though the *mens rea* necessary for criminal conviction is lacking a civil case may yet succeed since liability is established on the balance of probabilities. This is a lesser standard than that applied in the criminal courts where the case must be proved beyond reasonable doubt. Of course, raising a civil action in assault is in no sense dependent upon any criminal proceedings.

While it is clear that reparation can be sought in respect of invasions of bodily integrity the essence of this delict is not so much physical harm as insult or affront to dignity. The Scots approach derives from the *actio injuriarum* of Roman law which provided remedies in respect of a broad range of affronts and insults covering not only verbal injury, but also such matters as physical assault, affronts to a woman's modesty including stalking and making improper suggestions, and interfering with freedom of movement in public places.

It is argued that in Scots Law the *actio injuriarum* provides a basis from which a general right to reparation for invasions of personality could be derived. An example can be seen in *Henderson v Chief Constable of Fife Police* in which striking laboratory workers at the Victoria Hospital in Kirkcaldy were taken into police custody. One male pursuer recovered damages, because he was unjustifiably handcuffed. A female pursuer recovered, because she was required to remove her bra. It is not unusual for persons admitted to police cells to be asked to hand over ties or shoelaces in order to prevent them from hanging themselves. However, in this instance, where the pursuer was co-operative and there was no suggestion that she would seek to harm herself, it was held that the removal of her bra constituted an unjustifiable infringement of her liberty.

The recognition of rights of personality and availability in Scots law of solatium for affront enables the courts to provide damages in cases where there has been no physical harm. Scots law is not constrained as English law is by the difficulty in recognising new torts. It has been argued that the House of Lords decision in the English case of *Wainwright v Home Office*, in which the Court was unable to award damages in respect of distress and humiliation caused by a strip search, should not be followed in Scotland, principally because Scots law recognises such harm as reparable loss. In England this case did not fall within the confines of a recognised tort. The contrary argument, that

Wainright would be followed in Scotland, has also been put so clearly this is a matter of controversy.

Liability in assault is based on intention. Accidentally inflicted injuries are not actionable in assault. It is important to note that it is not necessary to establish the intention to harm the victim, only that the harmful act was intentional in the sense of being deliberately carried out. In delictual liability motive is, with very few exceptions, irrelevant. This is made abundantly clear by the case of *Reid v Mitchell* in which a farm worker fell from a hay cart as a result of "larking about" by his fellow workers.

Physical injury or even contact is not a necessary requirement for liability. In *Cock v Neville* a farmer was awarded a small sum of damages in respect of threats and abuse he had received from army officers trespassing on his land. In 1834 in *Tullis v Glenday* the sum of £40 in damages was awarded to the pursuer who alleged the defender had spat in his face. The sum claimed was £500! In *Ewing v Earl of Mar* it was held to amount to assault to ride a horse at a pedestrian causing danger and alarm and it was also insulting and an assault to spit at a person whether or not the spit landed on the victim.

To be actionable an assault must have been without the consent of the victim so complaints of assault are inapplicable, for example, in contact sports such as boxing or rugby where the invasion of physical integrity is part and parcel of the game. However, this limitation only applies so long as the rules of the game are adhered to. A boxer might be able to recover in respect of a below- the- belt injury, similarly a hooker who has had his ear bitten off by an opposing prop forward would have an action in delict for assault.

The action may be defended if it can be shown that the defender acted in self-defence or if the assault was the result of an unavoidable accident. As in the criminal law provocation does not provide a defence. Where established, provocation may operate as a mitigating factor to reduce any sum awarded in damages.

Seduction, Entrapment and Enticement

The essence of seduction is that deception or abuse of position has been used to gain a woman's consent to sexual intercourse. The critical element of this delict is fraud.

That seduction in the common sense of the word is not sufficient for liability is made clear in *Hislop v Ker*. The report states: "The Lords found a woman's being got with child was no ground of action for damages, else a hundred such processes would be intended by whores; as also they thought that every promise and insinuation of marriage was not sufficient to found this action, because these are made at such times very lightly; yet, on the other hand, such debauchery and fraudulent designs ought not to pass undiscouraged, therefore, in such a circumstantiate case, the Lords declared they would allow damages against the man who had *dolose* induced a party to trust him". The circumstances of the case were that the defender had induced the pursuer to go to great lengths in expectation of marriage. This included giving up her shop and moving house and was not restricted, as the report puts it: "to grant him the use of her body".

Seduction is seldom if ever litigated nowadays. This is partly a result of changing social mores. The extent to which defloration can be regarded in the modern context as a reparable loss must be limited. So far as pregnancy and childbirth are concerned there are now other legal means by which financial support may be secured, for example, through the offices of the Child Support Agency.

In considering reported cases from the nineteenth century it appears that the classic scenario for such a claim to arise was where masters took advantage of the youthful innocence of servant girls in order to lure them into the bedroom. Broken promises to marry also gave rise to delictual actions for seduction. While this delict is technically still operative, its main significance may be historical. On the other hand, since the essence of the delict is fraud the scope for future cases remains open.

Entrapment involves fraudulently inducing a person into a void marriage. Such actions arise occasionally, usually where the marriage is bigamous.

Enticement involves the unjustifiable enticement of a person away from their family. However, following the Law Reform (Husband and Wife) Scotland Act 1984, s.2(2) there is no longer liability in respect of a spouse enticed away from the marital home by a third party. This limits the modern scope of this delict. Because enticement must be unjustifiable it follows that there is no liability where a child is legally removed from the family for their protection or in the best interests of the child. For example, where a child is taken into care by the Local Authority acting in exercise of statutory powers or is legally removed by the police.

Where there is a case in enticement, the other family members may sue for damages in respect of loss of society. It has been suggested that enticement might provide a valid action where a child has been prevailed upon to leave the family to join a sect or cult.

Wrongful detention
The interest protected here is the liberty of the person. Nobody can be unlawfully detained against their will. The classic case of damages in respect of wrongful detention is *Mackenzie v Cluny Hill Hydropathic Company* in which a female guest was detained by the hotel manager in his office for some fifteen minutes. The pursuer was expected to apologise to two other guests whom she was alleged to have slighted. The pursuer successfully recovered damages in respect of the infringement of her liberty and affront.

Such instances of hotel managers taking upon themselves the role of a headteacher are thankfully rare. Complaints of wrongful detention are more likely to arise in connection with police activities. Scope for a successful case of wrongful arrest is limited. So long as police officers act within the law no claim in delict should arise. Where arrest is carried out without warrant, this may be justified on grounds of reasonable suspicion.

A suspected shoplifter may be detained for a reasonable time until the police arrive. However, following *Pringle v Bremner & Stirling* in order to evade liability suspicions must be reasonably held.

Harassment

Contravention of lawburrows is an old delict that is technically still competent. Indeed, a small number of twentieth century cases is reported (see, for example, *Liddle v Morton*). Where an individual anticipates harassment, violence or molestation, the delinquent may be called upon to lodge a sum of money known as caution with the court. In the event that lawburrows is contravened, that is, the cautioner harasses or molests the petitioner, the caution is forfeit. Lawburrows is a surviving relic of the period when there was no effective means of criminal law enforcement and the law of delict played a quasi-criminal role in keeping the peace.

Nowadays a person who fears harassment is much more likely to invoke the Protection from Harassment Act 1997. This statute was passed, partly as a response to the phenomenon of "stalking".

The victim may raise an action of harassment seeking damages from the perpetrator. Damages are recoverable both in respect of anxiety and any financial loss. It must be established that there has been harassment amounting to a course of conduct. Damages will not be granted in respect of an isolated event, there must have been harassment on at least two occasions. It must also be established that the defender's conduct was intended to amount to harassment or viewed objectively, may reasonably be interpreted in that way. Harassment is not statutorily defined.

The court may also make a non-harassment order, breach of which is a criminal offence.

Defences to an action of harassment are that the conduct was authorised by law; the conduct was pursued for the purposes of preventing or detecting crime; or the conduct was reasonable in the circumstances.

DELICTS AGAINST PROPERTY

Trespass and related delicts

There is a myth that there is no such thing as trespass in Scots Law. This is quite untrue. The point is that in contrast to England, no damages are available for a bare trespass. There must be actual damage before there can be reparation.

Historically, the idea of exclusive rights of possession of land did not gain ground until around the end of the eighteenth century by which time much land had been enclosed and land registration was sufficiently reliable. There was very little litigation prior to the nineteenth century and what little there was arose primarily from straying domestic animals and persons in pursuit of game. Stair did not consider trespass; Bell was the first institutional writer to accord it any detailed treatment.

Trespass is concerned with temporary and unjustifiable intrusions onto heritable property. The interest protected is the right to exclusive use and possession. Permanent physical intrusions such as walls, overhanging eaves or even branches are not trespass, but encroachment (see, for example, *Halkerston v Wedderburn*). Squatting is not trespass, but intrusion. Intrusion operates where the owner is not in possession at the time. Where the owner is ejected from the property this is yet another delict: ejection.

Heritable property is owned *a coelo usque ad centrum*, that is, from the sky to the centre of the earth so air space above the property is protected against trespass and encroachment. However, trespass may not be mobilised against over-flying aircraft by virtue of the Civil Aviation Act 1982, s.2. Trespass on moveable property that may be occupied, such as ships or oil rigs is actionable (see *Phestos Shipping Co Ltd v Kurimawan* and *Shell UK Ltd v McGillivray*.

While damages are available in respect of tangible harm done, for example, to crops, the primary remedy against trespass is interdict. Interdict is a discretionary remedy and will only be awarded in circumstances that are deemed appropriate. Interdict may be refused, for example, because of the triviality of the invasion complained of. The most famous case is *Winans v MacRae* in which the owner of 200,000 acres of deer forest was refused interdict to prevent a pet lamb from straying onto his land.

For an award of interdict there must be reasonable apprehension that future trespass will occur (see, for example, *Hay's Trustees v Young*). Interdict is personal and is only effective against persons named on the petition. An interdict against one person will not be effective against another who is not named. Interdict may be effective in cases of sit-ins in industrial disputes. For example, in *Caterpillar (UK) Ltd* interdict was granted against 808 named individuals. In other circumstances it may be impossible to identify the relevant individuals (see, for example, *Stirling Crawfurd v Clyde Navigation Trustees*). It has been observed that interdict in trespass is only truly effective against persistent identifiable individuals.

While proprietors can take precautionary measures to protect their privacy it is highly doubtful whether reasonable force can be used to eject trespassers. While Bell considered that the use of man traps was legitimate (para.961) this is clearly not the case in the modern law in which a duty of care is owed to trespassers under the Occupiers' Liability (Scotland) Act. Cases that have been founded upon to support a right to reasonable use of force, *Bell v Shand*, *Aitchison v Thorburn* and *Wood v North British Railway* do not support the use of force except where, as in

Wood, it is explicitly sanctioned by statute. The use of force is likely to give rise to liability in assault.

The most significant development in the law has been the coming into force of Statutory Access Rights under the Land Reform (Scotland) Act 2003. This Act creates extensive statutory rights to enter land belonging to others. It also imposes a regulatory regime which is likely to interact with common law remedies against trespass.

Section 1 provides everybody with two distinct rights. One is the right to be on land for specified purposes of recreation, educational activities or commercial enterprises. The other is the right to cross land. These rights only exist to the extent that they are exercised responsibly (s.2). Under s.28 the existence and extent of access rights and questions of responsibility may be determined by the sheriff court on summary application.

Land excepted from statutory access rights is defined in ss.6 and 7. For example, access rights may not be exercised in buildings or in the curtilage of buildings although curtilage is undefined. Equally land around houses sufficient to provide the occupants with a reasonable measure of privacy is excluded. There is a right to cross golf courses, but the greens are excluded from access rights under s.7(7)(b).

Certain activities are specifically excluded under s.9. Local Authorities have the power to regulate access under ss.11–27. The responsibilities of landowners and persons exercising access rights are set out in the Access Code drawn up by Scottish Natural Heritage (*www.outdooraccess-scotland.com*). This code does not have the force of law, but has evidentiary value. Responsible access is summarised in the code in the following terms: "take responsibility for your own actions; respect people's privacy and peace of mind, help land managers and others to work safely and effectively; care for your environment; keep your dog under proper control; and take extra care if you are organising an event or running a business".

The code also provides a long list of activities that are deemed "recreational" within the meaning of the Act. These include watching wildlife, sightseeing, painting and photography and family and social activities such as dog walking, picnics and sledging. Also listed are active pursuits such as climbing, caving, canoeing and wild camping. It has been observed that the code does not note whether sex is a recreational purpose within the meaning of the Act. Educational purposes under the Act would include visiting historic sights and geology field trips. Relevant commercial activities include mountain guiding or survival courses undertaken for profit, but not extractive industry!

Clearly rights may now be exercised over much land where previously people could have been excluded by interdict. It must be noted that the exclusions are complicated and the question over whether rights are exercised responsibly may give rise to difficulty. It may be thought that interdict will remain a competent remedy where persons enter land that is unambiguously excluded or where behaviour is clearly not responsible under the Act. Where either or both of these points are arguable then it remains to be seen whether interdicts will be granted in circumstances where petitioners have not first sought a declaratory ruling under s.28. Certainly in the past courts have refused interdict in circumstances where alternative remedial measures have not been implemented (see, for example, *Paterson v McPherson* and *Campbell v Mackay*). It is thought that the statutory mechanisms for regulating access may have to be exhausted before the common law remedy is granted.

Certain forms of trespass are criminal acts. For example, under the Trespass (Scotland) Act 1868 s.3(1) camping on land without permission or lighting a fire is punishable. However, under sch.2 of the Land Reform Act these no longer amount to offences where statutory access rights are exercised. Section 61 of the Criminal Justice and Public Order Act 1994 creates an offence where a common purpose has been formed to reside on land or where threatening, abusive or insulting behaviour has been used towards the occupier, his family or agents. This is collective trespass. It operates with a minimum of two trespassers and the necessary first step is for the occupier to take reasonable steps to ask the trespassers to leave. The police have powers to remove collective trespassers. Return to the land within three months or a failure to remove when required to do so is an offence.

In cases of a single trespasser damage to land may amount to vandalism. Threatening abusive or insulting behaviour is a breach of the peace. Specific forms of damage may amount to offences under other statutes, such as the Wildlife and Countryside Act 1981 or the Environmental Protection Act 1990. Driving a vehicle off road without permission is specifically excluded from statutory access rights under s.9(f) and is an offence under s.34 of the Road Traffic Act 1988.

The most important common law defence to trespass is justification. By definition a trespass is an unjustifiable intrusion so where there is justification there is no trespass. It is accepted, for instance that there is no trespass where land is entered to apprehend a criminal or to fight a fire. Furthermore there are many instances in which entering land is authorised by statute. Acquiescence also provides a defence. Consent to enter land may be express or implied, but consent, once given, can always be withdrawn (see, for example, *Steuart v Stephen* and *Love-Lee v Cameron of Locheil*).

Use of land *in aemulationem vicini*

This delict is broadly similar to nuisance although it pre-dates nuisance in Scots law considerably. It means spiteful or malicious use of land with the intention of causing harm to a neighbour. The relevant category of *culpa* is malice. Accordingly, the motive of the defender is relevant.

In order for malice to be inferred it must be clear that the predominant purpose of the activity complained of was to harm or annoy. Therefore if the defender can establish that the offensive act was conducted for their own convenience or benefit and that harm to the pursuer was merely consequential, then an action *in aemulationem* will be defeated (see, for example, *Dewar v Fraser*). In such circumstances a claim in nuisance would be more appropriate since nuisance does not require malice.

Examples of cases in which *aemulatio* was successfully pled include *Campbell v Muir* and *More v Boyle*. In the former, petitioner and respondent were neighbouring proprietors on opposite banks of the river Awe. The respondent moored his boat in the middle of the river and cast his rod in such a way as to prevent Sir Robert Usher who had leased the fishing rights from the petitioner, from continuing to fish. Sir Robert had been fishing at that spot for five minutes before the arrival of Muir. The pool where the men were fishing was some 60 yards wide by 146 yards long. Therefore there was plenty of space for Muir to fish the pool without interfering with Sir Robert. The case *in aemulationem* was established.

In *More v Boyle* the defender severed a water connection in his back garden in order to "get his own back" on neighbours who had refused to pay for a repair on the water pipe. The case *in aemulationem* was held relevant.

Wrongful interference with moveable property
The law of delict in this area is somewhat obscure, particularly since the continuing relevance of the old delict of spuilzie is highly debatable. Bankton described spuilzie as "the violent seizing, or unlawful taking possession of goods from another, without his consent or order of law, for lucre's sake." Originally spuilzie provided a remedy against violent dispossession or theft under which the goods would be restored to their lawful possessor. Spuilzie came also to deal with technical wrongs such as wrongfully withholding goods, for example, under a poinding without judicial warrant. Although originating as early as 1318 litigation in spuilzie was at a peak from the fifteenth to the seventeenth centuries.

Twentieth century attempts to revive spuilzie have contributed more confusion than clarity to the law. Examples of cases in which spuilzie has been discussed include: *FC Finance Ltd v Brown & Son*; *Mercantile Credit Company Ltd v Townsley*; *Harris v Abbey National plc*; and *Gemmell v Bank of Scotland*.

The Scottish Law Commission (Memorandum 31, 1976) suggested that the action of spuilzie was in need of radical reform. They also stated that: "[T]he invocation of ancient remedies of uncertain scope is not necessarily the ideal solution for modern wrongs". Indeed, wrongful interference with moveable property can normally be dealt with by other means, by simple application of the principle of *culpa*, by negligence, by the law of property or by the principles of restitution.

FRAUD AND THE ECONOMIC DELICTS

Fraud

Erskine's definition of fraud is: "a machination or contrivance to deceive". Fraud is established where an untrue statement or representation is made or where the statement is believed to be untrue or where the person making the statement is recklessly indifferent whether it be true or false.

Fraud is an intentional delict. It is important to note that the restrictions on recovery of pure economic loss that apply in unintentional or negligent wrongdoing do not apply in intentional delicts. Of course, the form of loss to which fraud is most likely to give rise is economic.

Fraud arises most often in the context of misrepresentation inducing another party to contract. In such circumstances fraud gives rise to both delictual and contractual remedies. For example, in the case of *Smith v Sim* the pursuer bought a pub in Montrose relying on turnover figures produced by the defender. The figures turned out to be fraudulent. Under the law of contract Smith had the right to have the contract reduced. The fact that he chose not to exercise this right did not preclude him from recovering damages in delict in respect of fraud.

Passing off

Broadly, passing off is an attempt by a trader to appropriate the goodwill of another trader. This occurs where the name or "get up" of a product is sufficiently similar to another product to amount to a misrepresentation that will confuse consumers. Loss is in the form of reduced sales or damaged reputation.

A fictitious, but clear illustration that may be familiar to readers is found in the Eddie Murphy movie "Coming to America" in which the father of the heroine operates a burger outlet called McDowall's. The "M" is crafted so as to be identical to the "M" used by McDonald's although McDowall maintains that his M is made up of golden arcs as opposed to McDonald's golden arches.

The example shows all the essential elements of passing off as laid down by Lord Diplock in *Erven Warninck BV v J Townend & Sons (Hull) Ltd*. First, there is a misrepresentation. Secondly, the misrepresentation is made by a trader in the course of trade. Thirdly, the misrepresentation is made to prospective customers of his or ultimate consumers of goods and services provided by him. Fourthly, the misrepresentation is calculated to injure the business or goodwill of another trader. Fifthly, the misrepresentation has caused or probably will cause damage to the business or goodwill of the other trader.

In our example it is probable that McDowall sought to benefit from McDonald's goodwill. His motivation was to benefit himself rather than to harm McDonald's. However he cannot evade liability on this basis. If harm to McDonald's is reasonably foreseeable then the requirements for liability can be satisfied. Harm to McDonald's arises, either because customers go to McDowall's in the mistaken belief that they are eating at McDonald's or because, having eaten at McDowall's they foreswear burgers for life!

The primary remedy in cases of passing off is interdict. Damages may also be available although the process of quantifying loss may present problems.

Breach of confidence
It is a delict to publish or otherwise disseminate information provided in confidence or information gained from a relationship of confidence. In the commercial context trade secrets may be protected by the law of contract. Restrictive covenants forbidding divulgence of sensitive business information are enforceable to the extent that they are reasonably necessary.

However, breach of confidence is not restricted to the commercial context. An obligation to maintain confidentiality may arise in circumstances as diverse as employment in the secret service where divulgence of information might threaten national security on the one hand and between married partners or even lovers on the other. An obligation of confidentiality clearly arises between banker and client, solicitor and client or between doctor and patient. The obligation arises wherever there is a relationship of confidence irrespective of whether there is a contractual relationship.

Both parties to the relationship are bound by the obligation. The obligation also extends to any third party to whom one of the parties has divulged information. Thus if the editor of a newspaper publishes information that is known to be confidential or that a reasonable person would know should be confidential in the circumstances then liability in delict will arise (see *Lord Advocate v Scotsman Publications Ltd*).

The primary remedy is interdict to prevent dissemination of information. Damages may be recoverable although depending on the circumstances damages may be difficult to assess. In the "spycatcher" case, *Attorney-General v Times Newspapers*, the editor of the Sunday Times was liable to account for profits following publication of confidential information.

Inducing / procuring breach of contract
It is an actionable delict if a person induces another to breach a contract to which they are party. This is a relatively recent delict recognised by Sots law in the case of *British Motor Trade Association v Gray*. Inducing a breach of contract is a wrong in itself. In order to be actionable the means used does not have to be unlawful. The innocent party to the contract can sue the party who induces the breach in delict. Of course, they may also sue the other party to the contract for breach. Before damages can be awarded there must be loss. However, where breach has been induced

courts will have little difficulty in inferring loss. Scottish courts require knowledge of the contract before a person can be held liable for inducing breach. The strong suggestion from the case of *Rossleigh Ltd v Leader Cars Ltd* is that actual knowledge of the existence of a contract is required although the specific terms of the contract need not be known.

Inducing breach of contract deals with the situation where the delinquent is able to prevail on one party to the contract, perhaps by threats, perhaps by financial inducement to breach. Procurement refers to the situation where the delinquent is able to engineer a breach of contract where the party is unwilling to breach. This can be done directly, for example, by vandalising machinery essential to performance of the contract or indirectly, for example, by inducing a breach of contract on the part of a supplier. In contrast to inducing breach of contract, liability only arises in respect of procurement where unlawful means are used to procure the breach.

Wrongful interference with performance of contract
This arises as an actionable wrong where a third party interferes with a contract in a way which falls short of producing a technical breach. This is a development on the delict of inducing breach arising from the case of *Torquay Hotel Co Ltd v Cousins*. Direct interference will give rise to liability whether or not unlawful means are used. Indirect interference will only give rise to liability where unlawful means are employed.

Wrongful interference with trade
It has been argued that economic delicts such as wrongful interference with contract and inducing and procuring breach should be subsumed under the broader heading of wrongful interference with trade. This approach derives from the English case of *Lonrho plc v Fayed* and is to some extent supported in Scots law by *Shell UK Ltd v McGillivray*. The requirements of this new delict call for intention to harm and actual loss caused by unlawful means.

Intimidation
This delict derives from the House of Lords case of *Rookes v Barnard*. It arises where one party threatens a second with an unlawful act unless the second party causes economic harm to a third party. In *Rookes* three trade union officials threatened their employer, BOAC with unlawful strike action unless Rookes' employment was terminated. Rookes succeeded in his case against the three officials.

Conspiracy
The delict of conspiracy requires a combination of parties acting together to cause economic harm to another party. If parties act together with the predominant motive of causing harm to another then liability in delict arises whether or not the means used to inflict harm are unlawful. It may

be noted that this is one of the rare instances in delictual liability in which motive is relevant.

Thus while it is not an actionable delict for a business to attempt to drive another concern out of business, for example, by undercutting prices, (see *Allen v Flood*) where two or more business or parties combine with the intention of causing economic harm then delictual liability arises. So a course of action that would not be delictual if carried out by a single party becomes delictual by virtue of conspiracy. Where the means used are lawful and the predominant motive behind any course of action is to benefit the participating parties and intention to cause harm to the pursuer is absent then no delict is committed. This follows from *Crofter Hand Woven Harris Tweed Co Ltd v Veitch*. The onus is on the pursuer to establish predominant motive to harm. The pursuer must also establish economic loss. Where the means used are unlawful, in the sense of being criminal, in breach of contract, in breach of statute or delictual, then the pursuer has to establish that the conspirators intended harm. They do not have to show that harm was the predominant motive for the acts.

---

10. REMEDIES

INTRODUCTION

Generally where loss is caused by a wrong, the law provides a remedy. Where the loss is quantifiable in money terms the remedy sought will usually be damages. However, depending on the circumstances, other remedies may be more appropriate.

The simplest remedy is self-help. Clearly the scope of self-help is limited. Its most clear application is in trespass. A landowner may construct a fence or dyke to keep other people or animals from straying onto their property. Trespassers may be asked to leave, but it is highly doubtful if force may be used to eject persons from premises or land. Trees or shrubs that encroach on land, for example, branches that overhang one's property, may be lopped or pruned with no right of recourse accruing to the owner.

A person who has been wronged may seek declarator. A declarator is given when a state of affairs amounting to a delict is found to exist. For example, a declarator may provide that a state of affairs amounts to a nuisance. Normally an action for declarator will be accompanied by a plea for damages or interdict since the award of declarator itself does not compel the defender to do anything, to refrain from doing anything or to pay anything. It is simply a statement of the legal position of the parties. A declarator may be useful to prevent the running of prescription and in nuisance it will defeat a later defence of acquiescence.

The principal remedies are interdict and damages. These are both complicated and entire books have been devoted to consideration of each. The following text is an outline guide to the essential points only.

INTERDICT

The essence of interdict is that prevention is better than cure. Interdict is sought to prevent an anticipated wrong or to put an end to a continuing wrong. An interdict restrains the activities of the party against whom it is awarded. In short, it forbids the party interdicted from conducting the activity specified. If the terms of the interdict are breached, the party in breach will be liable to a fine or imprisonment. The party seeking the interdict is the petitioner. The party against whom the interdict is sought is the respondent.

Interdict is broadly equivalent to the English remedy of injunction. The use of the term injunction is inappropriate in Scotland. Beware of loose usage by newsreaders and suchlike. When an injunction is awarded by the English courts, for example, against publication or distribution of memoirs in breach of the Official Secrets Act, it has proved necessary to seek separately, an interdict in the Court of Session, so that the Scottish media also is restrained from publication.

Interdict has no real application in negligence. Interdict is an appropriate remedy in delicts of intention, for example, in defamation, trespass, nuisance and use of land *in aemulationem vicini*. Interdict is used to protect intellectual property rights and is generally applicable in the economic delicts such as passing off or wrongful interference with contracts.

Interdicts must be framed in clear and precise terms so that the party interdicted should be left in no doubt regarding the forbidden activity. The terms of the interdict must be no wider than necessary to curb the wrong complained of.

Interdicts may be permanent, that is, made without limit of time, or interim. An interim interdict is an immediate remedy that may be applied for at any stage in the process of application for a permanent interdict. For example, if an interdict is sought to prevent publication of defamatory material in a newspaper an interim interdict may be required if intended publication is imminent. The award of a permanent interdict requires more time and justification and will not help the petitioner if the material is published before the court reaches a conclusion. The interim interdict serves the purpose of preventing publication while the more detailed consideration required for permanent interdict takes place.

Interim interdicts are awarded at the court's discretion. There must be a *prima facie* case, in other words on the basis of the petitioner's pleadings it must appear that a relevant case in defamation, or nuisance or whatever wrong is complained of has been made out. The court will then consider the balance of convenience between the parties. For example, it may be argued that the award of interdict will cause a greater wrong to the respondent than the wrong complained of by the petitioner. Any public interest in the activity complained of will be taken into account by the court. Only where the balance of convenience is held to be in the petitioner's favour will interim interdict be granted. An interim interdict is valid until recalled by the court.

In general interdict is only awarded where there is a genuine prospect of future wrongs. Interdict is not competent in respect of an activity that is unlikely to be repeated.

DAMAGES

The purpose of damages is to repair the loss suffered by the pursuer. Damages in Scots law are not intended to penalise and do not reflect the degree of culpability of the delinquent party. In awarding damages the courts seek, insofar as is possible, to effect *restitutio in integrum*. That is, to restore the pursuer to the position they would have been in had the delict not occurred.

Broadly, claims for damages fall under two heads, solatium, and patrimonial loss. In cases of personal injury solatium is awarded in respect of pain and suffering. Solatium is also awarded in respect of affront, for example, in defamation. It is helpful to distinguish the two forms of solatium. The expression "patrimonial" derives from the Roman concept of *patrimonium* meaning a person's estate. Patrimonial loss covers all tangible economic losses including property damage and financial harm. Medical expenses consequent on personal injury count as patrimonial losses.

Where the harm sustained is property damage the process of assessing the quantum (amount) of damages is relatively straightforward. The pursuer may recover from the defender the cost of repairing or replacing the property. There may be derivative losses that are also recoverable in damages, so if a car is damaged through negligence the defender may be held liable to pay the costs of a hire car while the original vehicle is being fixed.

Damages in personal injury cases

Where the pursuer has suffered personal injury the claim for damages in respect of pain and suffering will be under the head of solatium and any derivative losses will be claimed under the head of patrimonial loss.

Placing a monetary value on pain and suffering is an inexact science. The severity and nature of the injuries will be taken into account along with the extent of any disability or loss of amenity. Awareness of pain is relevant, so if the pursuer is in a coma there may be no award of solatium. Anything which reduces the pursuer's enjoyment of life, including pain and suffering caused by the realisation of reduced life expectancy will be taken into consideration. In practice, close regard is paid to the sums awarded in previous decisions and lawyers make great use of McEwan and Paton's looseleaf guide. By using this guide it is possible to find out recent awards made in respect of particular injuries. For example, if a client has lost a leg the guide will give details of sums awarded in previous instances of the same injury.

Solatium may be awarded, not only in respect of pain and suffering from the date of injury to the date of proof, but also in respect of future pain and suffering where this is relevant. Where the victim has died immediate relatives may claim in respect of: distress and anxiety caused by the victim's suffering while still alive; grief and sorrow caused by death; and loss of the victim's society.

Damages in respect of patrimonial loss cover loss of earnings, outlays and reasonable expenses. A sum may be awarded in respect of necessary services rendered by relatives under the Administration of Justice Act 1982, s.8. Section 9 of the same Act provides that a sum may be awarded to relatives in respect of services that the victim is no longer able, on account of their injuries, to render the family. This would include such things as vehicle maintenance, childcare and housework. Where the victim has died relatives may also recover damages in respect of loss of support and funeral expenses.

Patrimonial loss is subdivided under two further heads, past and future of which future loss is both the most important and most difficult to calculate. The pursuer may claim for loss of earnings up until the date of proof. The sum payable is net wages or salary. To calculate future earnings the net wage at the date of proof is taken as the mutiplicand. The court must determine the number of years over which damages are due in respect of future earnings. This is the multiplier. The multiplier is never as great as the number of years the pursuer has left until retirement. The product of the multiplicand and multiplier is then calculated to give a lump sum that can then be invested. Expenses such as the cost of nursing care can be taken into account under future losses.

Awards of damages, both past and future are subject to the payment of interest.

Deductions

Damages in respect of patrimonial loss are subject to deductions. Earnings or remuneration from an employer, unemployment benefits prior to the date of the award of damages and any benevolent payment made by the person responsible for the injury should all be taken into account in reducing the award of damages.

Under the Social Security (Recovery of Benefits) Act 1997 various social security benefits paid to the defender during the "relevant period" must be deducted from the sum payable to the pursuer by the person against whom the award has been made, the compensator. The "relevant period" is five years from the date of the accident or five years from first claiming benefit in respect of "a disease". Where damages are paid within five years of the accident, the relevant period ends at the date of payment. The sum deducted by the compensator from the victim's compensation is then paid directly to the Secretary of State.

Provisional Damages

Where it is proved or admitted that there is a risk that the pursuer's health or condition will seriously deteriorate in the future the Administration of Justice Act 1982, s.12 provides that a provisional award of damages may be made. Such an award is only permissible where the defender is a public authority or is insured. A provisional award of damages means that the pursuer may seek further damages in future if the risk of serious deterioration materialises. At that stage it will be possible to assess the extent of pain and suffering or any reasonable expenses. It is within the discretion of the court to set a time limit against future claims.

Interim Damages

The court may grant an award of interim damages before the process of litigation is concluded. Interim payments will only be awarded where liability is admitted by the defender or where there appears no question that the pursuer will succeed. This means also that there should no prospect of a substantial reduction of damages on grounds of contributory negligence.

APPENDIX: SAMPLE EXAMINATION QUESTIONS AND ANSWER PLANS

Question
Senga McGlumpher asks her building society to instruct a surveyor to conduct a detailed structural survey on a house that she is considering buying. The building society instructs a firm of surveyors, Bobbit & Co to conduct a full structural survey on behalf of a Ms McGlumpher. The survey is conducted and the report concludes that the building is sound.

It transpires that Senga cannot afford to increase her mortgage. However her sister Edna is interested in the property and Senga gives Edna the survey on condition that Edna pay the surveyor's invoice. Edna settles the bill. In reliance on the survey Edna buys the house. The house turns out to suffer badly from rising damp that will cost £10,000 to put right. Edna contacts Bobbit & Co who appear willing to discuss compensation with her.

Advise Bobbit & Co.

Notes for answer
There is a defect in the quality of Edna's house. She has suffered pure economic loss. Ought Bobbit & Co to compensate her? This issue has to be determined according to the principles of *Hedley Byrne v Heller*. Can the requirements of proximity be satisfied? In circumstances of a full structural survey you can presume that there has been an assumption of responsibility on the part of Bobbit & Co. If you want to impress the examiner by a brief but relevant foray into the law of contract you may note that while it is possible to avoid liability by use of a contractual term, where a full structural survey has been instructed it is unlikely that a court would uphold any such term as reasonable within the meaning of the Unfair Contract Terms Act 1977. There is no mention of any such term or disclaimer of responsibility in the text so an answer that does not consider the issue is fine, but there should be some mention of assumption of responsibility since that is a *Hedley Byrne* requirement.

Edna appears to have relied on the exercise of due care by Bobbit & Co and since they are surveyors her reliance is reasonable. The problem bears a superficial resemblance to *Martin v Bell Ingram* in which the pursuer did recover damages in respect of a negligently conducted survey, but there is an important distinguishing feature here that you should spot. Our case is distinguishable on the basis that the party who relied upon the survey was not the person on whose behalf the survey was conducted. The particular transaction was the same, the purchase of the house that was the subject of the survey, but the identity of Edna was unknown to Bobbit & Co. Therefore Edna's case falls foul of *Caparo v Dickman*. To be liable Bobbit would have to have known that Edna herself would rely on their survey. The relationship between Edna and Bobbit & Co is insufficiently proximate for a duty of care to avoid causing pure economic loss to arise.

Apparently Bobbit & Co do not realise that the Ms McGlumpher who is seeking compensation is not the Ms McGlumpher upon whose behalf the survey was conducted. The fact that Edna has settled Senga's bill is irrelevant. Edna has fulfilled Senga's contractual obligation, but this does not mean that Bobbit & Co owe Edna any obligation in delict. You have been asked to advise Bobbit & Co. Forget any sympathy you may have with the unfortunate Edna and act like a professional. Advise Bobbit & Co that they are not obliged to compensate Edna. If, as a matter of commercial practice, they decide to compensate Edna to some extent that is up to them. The point is that they are under no obligation.

Question

Bill is the manager of a foundry. He hears cries and a commotion coming from a part of the foundry one hundred metres away. When he goes to investigate he discovers that there has been a spillage of molten metal and sees two men wrapping a third in a fire blanket. He can see that the victim's clothes are burning. He does not recognise the victim since his face is badly burnt and his hair has gone. He is screaming. At that point a crucible fractures and Bill and the two helpers spring away. The eruption of molten metal engulfs the original victim who burns to death. It dawns on Bill that the victim is his brother-in-law. As a result of the incident Bill suffers clinical depression and insomnia. When he does sleep nightmares awaken him.

The Foundry owners admit that the incident occurred as a result of their negligence, but they deny that they owed Bill a duty of care in respect of psychiatric harm. Can Bill recover damages?

Notes for answer

Clearly Bill has suffered loss in the form of a recognised psychiatric illness so the requirements of *Simpson v ICI* are satisfied. The issue here is whether Bill should sue as a primary or a secondary victim. Since both appear possible from the text you should consider both possibilities and evaluate Bill's chances of recovering damages in each.

Applying *Page v Smith* Bill can recover damages as a primary victim provided he was within the area of potential harm. The fact that he incurred no physical injury is irrelevant since it is clear that provided a duty not to cause physical harm is breached the victim can recover damages even though the harm that results is psychiatric.

You might like to illustrate the application of *Page v Smith* and the importance attached to being in physical danger by reference to *White v Chief Constable of South Yorkshire, Hale v London Underground, Young v Charles Church* and *Hunter v British Coal*. However there are potential pitfalls. It is critical that you cite *Page v Smith* in your answer since that is the source of the rule that you are applying. The other cases largely serve to illustrate the application of that rule. Failing *Page v Smith* the next best case upon which to base your answer is *White* since that too is a decision of the House of Lords. If you go into too much detail on all the case law there is a danger that you will not have time to give proper consideration to the whole question or the rest of the exam paper. When discussing case law it is vital to show why you think any given case is relevant to the issue under consideration. All these cases are clearly relevant to the issue that is being discussed so they may be considered, but make sure your answer addresses the question. Sometimes students feel that the object of an exam is to demonstrate that they know the facts and decision in 100 cases. Knowledge of case law is laudable, but it will not gain you good grades if you discuss cases at the expense of answering the question set. The question every student wants and no examiner ever sets is "Write all you know about.....(e.g.) the recovery of damages for psychiatric harm in negligence." If you solve the problem identifying and applying the appropriate rule and preferably the correct source of the rule then you will do fine. If you can embellish your answer by a broader discussion of the case law that is clearly related to the issues raised by the problem then so much the better.

Whether Bill can recover as a primary victim will depend upon his ability to establish that he was within the area of potential danger when the second spillage occurred. The text appears to suggest that he was.

In order to recover as a secondary victim Bill will have to satisfy the requirements set out in *Alcock v Chief Constable of South Yorkshire*. Clearly Bill was present during the second incident and witnessed the immediate aftermath of the first with his own senses. Bill must establish close ties of love and affection with his brother in law and he will have to lead evidence to prove this. You do not know whether Bill will be able to prove this or not, but you might conclude that the requirement of a close tie of love and affection presents a barrier to recovery as a secondary victim that does not apply to Bill's case as a primary victim. If Bill cannot prove close ties of love and affection to the satisfaction of the court then he may still recover damages as a primary victim provided the court is satisfied that he was within the area of potential danger.

Question

Horace is travelling by train. The train is crowded and Horace has to stand by the door. There is a notice above the door warning passengers that it is dangerous to lean against the door or out of the window while the train is in motion. The door locks are controlled by a master switch in the driver's compartment. When the train leaves the station Bob the driver forgets to flick the switch. Bob's train is running late and he drives much faster than usual in order to make up time. When travelling fast round a bend the standing passengers are thrown outwards. Most have found something to hold onto, but a large man standing in front of Horace has found no support and he is thrown against Horace. The door opens and Horace falls onto the track. Horace's spine is severed at the neck, but he is not dead. The door slams shut as the train immediately enters a bend in the other direction and nobody realises Horace is gone so nobody pulls the communication cord to stop the train.

A thief sees Horace and rifles his pockets. He takes Horace's wallet and proceeds fraudulently to use Horace's credit cards. Debts of several thousand pounds are incurred. This loss is not covered by any card protection plan or other insurance. The credit card companies are entitled under contract to hold Horace liable for these debts. The thief is never caught.

Finally Horace is taken to hospital. He lives, but is paraplegic. His career as a solicitor is at an end. He is no longer able to do odd jobs around the house or to cook for his family, a task which has generally fallen to him in the past since he enjoys cooking and his wife does not. These tasks are now performed by his father who also provides nursing care.

You are asked to advise Horace regarding the possibility of recovering his losses. You also need to advise him of possible defences against his claim.

Notes for answer

A question of this nature involves several issues. You are being assessed, not only on your knowledge of the law, but on your ability to provide an analysis. Take time to read the text carefully and plan a structured answer around the issues that arise. The first task is to identify the issues and it may be a good idea to set these out in an introductory paragraph before examining the issues in turn.

Clearly the problem involves negligence. In any problem involving negligence you should consider the existence of a duty of care, the standard of care applicable, whether the duty was breached, causation and remoteness of damage. You need not give each of these aspects equal weight. In this problem the existence of a duty, the standard of care and breach are pretty straightforward. More detailed consideration has to be given the issues of causation and remoteness of damage. The text also raises the issue of vicarious liability. In addition, because the text provides some detail on the types of loss suffered by the victim you should consider what may be claimed under different heads of damages. Finally, you will need to consider possible defences to the action since you have been asked to do so.

Horace may be advised to raise an action in negligence against the railway company. It is clear that the negligent act or omission occurred in the course of Bob's employment. Therefore his employers will be vicariously liable. Authority on this point may be cited such as *Kirby v*

NCB. The point is simple and there is no difficulty in applying the general rule so there should be no need to embark on a lengthy discussion of the case law. Horace may elect to sue Bob either instead of or as well as the railway company. Liability is joint and several. In practice Horace would probably name both as defenders in his action, but would have more hope of recovering damages from the railway company than from Bob.

There can be no doubt that a duty of care is owed Horace by Bob. Passengers on a train are owed a duty of care under s.2(1) Occupiers' Liability (Scotland) Act. Horace should have no difficulty in establishing breach of the standard of care since Bob has neglected to follow normal practice in implementing a safety system that is found in all modern trains in this country. Bob has made a negligent omission. Bob may also have been negligent or possibly reckless in driving a crowded train so fast. If so this is a negligent act, it may indeed be reckless. You can't tell from the text whether his speed was excessive in terms of the margins of safety for the particular section of track. However the clear implication to be drawn from the text is that Bob was driving too fast.

Horace should be able to establish that an accident of the type he has suffered, *i.e.* falling out of the door, was a reasonably foreseeable consequence of Bob's failure to lock the doors, particularly in circumstances where a fast moving train is crowded to the extent that passengers are standing in the space between carriages. Certainly it is foreseeable that standing passengers will be thrown outwards when a train is driven fast round a corner. This is the effect of centrifugal force, but you are not being examined on physics! Having considered the cases of *Muir v Glasgow Corporation* and *Hughes v Lord Advocate* you can conclude that the requirements of foreseeability of harm are satisfied since an accident of this type was a foreseeable likelihood.

Horace will have to establish that his losses are directly attributable to the Bob's negligence. Horace has suffered two forms of loss. He has incurred personal injury and losses arising from personal injury on one hand and the loss of his wallet and consequent financial loss on the other. You need to consider these losses separately. Deal with personal injury first.

Bob's negligence is the *causa sine qua non* of Horace's accident. Is it also the *causa causans*? The defenders may seek to argue that the direct and immediate cause of Horace falling out the door was the large man whose actions amounted to a *novus actus interveniens* breaking the chain of causation between the original negligent omission and the accident. You should identify and evaluate this potential argument.

A court would be unlikely to regard the action of the large man as a *novus actus interveniens*. This is because his loss of balance was an involuntary act caused by the movement of the train which was being driven too fast. The man's loss of balance was a reasonably foreseeable consequence of the motion of the train that was under Bob's control. Therefore the large man was an unwitting agent of Bob's negligence and not an independent actor. For this reason he cannot be held to have broken the causal chain between Bob's negligence and Horace's accident. Accordingly Bob's negligence is the *causa causans* of Horace's injuries.

This may be a good point at which to consider the other loss, that is, the loss arising from the theft of Horace's wallet. Since there is no prospect of recovering from the thief it must be considered whether this loss too can be recovered from Bob and the railway company. There are a number of reasons for answering this question in the negative. First, loss of this nature is not foreseeable as a reasonable and probable consequence of Bob's negligence so this claim should fall on the application of *Muir v Glasgow Corporation*. Indeed this loss is too remote. This claim also fails on causation. While Bob's negligence is the *causa sine qua non*, since but for it Horace would not have been lying injured in a place where he could be robbed, it is not the *causa causans* since the theft amounts to a *novus actus interveniens* breaking the causal link between Bob and the loss. The theft is a *novus actus interveniens*, because it is the independent act of a third party unconnected in any way with the original negligence. In this case the loss lies where it falls. In the circumstances it is possible that the credit companies may be persuaded to write off the debt.

Horace may be advised to seek solatium in respect of his pain, suffering, loss of amenity and any contemplation of loss of life expectancy. He would be able to recover damages in respect of services now provided by his father under the Administration of Justice (Scotland) Act, ss.8 and 9. Furthermore he would be able to recover damages in respect of loss of earnings. Since you are not provided with Horace's earnings in the text you may safely assume that you are not required to calculate a sum. To be on the safe side you might note that Horace's salary at the date of proof (the multiplicand) will be multiplied by a notional figure representing the years Horace had left to work, although the latter figure (the multiplier) will not be as great as the number of years until Horace was due to retire.

Horace is likely to succeed in his claim. There should be no reduction in damages for contributory negligence since there is nothing in the text to suggest that Horace contributed to his own injuries. Equally the defence of *volenti non fit injuria* will not succeed. While the notice warned of the dangers of leaning on the door, Hamish was not leaning on it, he was pushed against it. There is nothing to suggest that in getting on the train he consented to assume the risk that Bob would drive negligently.

Question

Maybeline and Nadine work for a firm of accountants. Maybeline feels bullied and harassed by one of the partners, Gloria, because Gloria behaves towards her in an utterly unreasonable fashion. The firm operate a grievance procedure. Maybeline fears that making a complaint will get her into more trouble. Nadine enters a complaint stating that Gloria is overbearing, rude and impatient and that she bullies Maybeline. On

Friday night in the pub Maybeline spends most of the evening bitching about Gloria to anyone who will listen. As the evening wears on the tales become grossly exaggerated and Maybeline makes various unfounded allegations about Gloria's slapdash approach to her work for clients in front of the local inspector of taxes.

The senior partner has a word with Gloria about the complaint made against her and word reaches her ears of the discussions in the pub. She intends suing both Maybeline and Nadine for damages in defamation. Will she be successful?

Notes for answer

The case against Maybeline appears clear. It appears that Maybeline has made false statements casting doubt upon Gloria's professional competence. Such allegations are generally accepted as defamatory so there should be little difficulty in establishing that what has been said about Gloria would lower her in the esteem of right thinking people, having applied Lord Akin's dictum in *Sim v Stretch*. Because the statements are false, intention on the part of Maybeline will be presumed.

Any case against Nadine is most unlikely to succeed. For one thing it is arguable whether the allegations she made against Gloria would amount to defamation if they were false. The comments were not pleasant, but could they bear a defamatory meaning? This is for you to consider and decide, but there is no obviously right answer. In any case the comments cannot satisfy the test for defamation since it appears from the text that nothing but the truth was communicated and a defamatory statement is by definition false. Truth (*veritas*) affords a complete defence. Moreover, having followed the correct procedure for raising complaints Nadine's comments attract the protection of qualified privilege. It may be easily inferred that Nadine made the complaint considering herself under a duty to do so. Since the grievance procedure was followed the comments would have been made to a person with an interest in hearing them. Certainly a senior partner has a legitimate interest in being told of serious difficulties in office relationships. All these factors point to the conclusion that Nadine's comments enjoy qualified privilege. Had the allegations been false and defamatory Gloria could not recover damages from Nadine in a defamation action unless she proved malice on Nadine's part. Since the allegations are true there is no case in defamation.

Question

Hilda moves into a new house. Her next door neighbour is Stan. Stan has been a keen pigeon fancier since he retired 10 years ago. Stan is widowed, he has no family and pigeons are his only pleasure. Hilda does not like birds and she has a particular antipathy towards pigeons. Hilda complains often to Stan about his pigeons. She complains that large numbers of them gather on her roof and that she cannot get her washing hung out for fear that it will be fouled by pigeon droppings. Eventually Hilda threatens to raise an action in nuisance seeking interdict to prevent Stan from keeping pigeons.

You are Stan's only friend and he seeks your advice.

Notes for answer

Clearly the facts resemble *Allison v Stevenson*. However in this case a court might well reach a different conclusion and refuse interdict. There are significant distinguishing factors. While the court has to balance the conflicting interests of neighbours, in *Allison* there was material harm caused to roans and drainpipes. Inconvenience has to be substantial before it becomes actionable and Hilda's complaints appear lacking in substance. This may be a case for applying the maxim, *lex non favet votis delicatorum*, the law does not favour the wishes of the fastidious. If it is the case that Hilda's washing gets covered in guano whenever she hangs it out to dry then her case may be strengthened. Even so it is not obvious that an interdict will be granted. Everyone knows that the odd bird dropping is a natural hazard of drying washing outdoors. The text is deliberately vague on whether Hilda's washing has actually suffered to any extent. Although Stan may feel that his behaviour in keeping pigeons is reasonable this is not really the point. The critical issue is whether the harm or inconvenience suffered by Hilda is more than reasonably tolerable (*Watt v Jamieson*). On the basis of the facts as set out in the text it must be highly doubtful whether the *plus quam tolerabile* test will be satisfied.

In the unlikely event that the court holds that the inconvenience suffered by Hilda amounts to nuisance Stan cannot defend the action by arguing that he and his pigeons were there first. It is no defence to state that the petitioner came to the nuisance (*Webster v Lord Advocate*). Furthermore Stan is not protected by prescription since he kept pigeons for only ten years and the prescriptive period is twenty (Prescription and Limitation (Scotland) Act 1973, s.7(1)).

You should advise Stan that it is most unlikely that he will have to give up his pigeons. Advise him to defend any action brought by Hilda on the basis that any inconvenience suffered by Hilda is insufficiently grave to amount to nuisance.

Question

Bob the builder is renovating flats above a museum. There is scaffolding placed against the building. Normally, great care is taken by Bob to ensure that no access to the flats can be gained. However, when the window frames have been removed two thieves enter the flats by night and gain access to the museum below by breaking through the ceiling from the flat above. They remove several items of value.

Is Bob liable to the trustees of the museum in respect of property damage and the value of the stolen items?

Notes for answer

The issue is whether Bob is liable for the acts of independent third parties, and particularly, does he owe the museum a duty of care? What is the governing authority? Probably not *Dorset Yacht Co v Home Office*, since there is no element of control exercised by Bob over the thieves, nor is there any assumption of responsibility. The thieves are truly independent in a way that the borstal boys were not.

Is Bob under a duty of care to the museum trustees in respect of the loss that has arisen? *Squires v Perth & Kinross DC* might suggest such a duty although the break in to the museum is arguably less foreseeable than a break in to a jewellers. However *Squires* might be viewed as superseded by House of Lords authority in the form of *Maloco v Littlewoods*.

There is scope for discussion although it is most likely that the view that will prevail is that there is no duty owed by a proprietor in respect of acts by independent third parties in such circumstances. This would follow from Lord Goff's speech in *Maloco* and would be in line with English decisions such as *Perl Exporters v Camden LBC*. *Aliter*, Lord McKay appeared to base his reasoning on foreseeability of harm and if that line is taken then it is possible that a different conclusion on the existence of a duty could be reached.

In other words there is no right answer, but the probable result is that there would be no duty owed.

Question

Does liability under the Occupiers' Liability (Scotland) Act 1960 arise in any of the following?

Q1. The local primary school has a flat roof. The school building is surrounded by an eight foot high wall although there are places where it is possible for a child aged nine or over to climb to gain access to the school yard. Children have been known to gain access to the school grounds during the summer holidays and have been seen on occasions to play on the roof. They are usually warned off by an adult. No child has ever suffered an accident on the roof.

On this occasion, during the school holidays, three boys aged 14 climb over the wall and gain access to the roof via a rhone pipe. They play tig during which they bounce off plastic skylights. One boy jumps onto a skylight from a height of five feet and crashes through it falling to his death in the school hall below. It is established in evidence that the school could have installed stronger skylights and boxed in the rhones at reasonable expense.

Q2. An Electricity company have surrounded a transformer with a high fence topped with barbed wire. There are also Danger High Voltage signs on display around the transformer. Nevertheless a 12-year-old boy manages to scale the fence and gains access to the transformer whereupon he is fried to death.

Q3. A Railway company have protected their railway line from trespassers by a fence made from old railway sleepers. Over the years gaps have appeared in the fence. Two fifteen-year-olds of opposing gender get through one of these gaps in order to cross the railway line to get to a derelict building for purposes that need no further elaboration. Unfortunately a train kills one and seriously injures the other.

Notes for answers

Q1. The facts in this problem are more or less identical to those in *Devlin v Strathclyde Regional Council*. That case should be followed. A duty is owed under s.2(1) of the Act to the boys, even though they are trespassers. Their presence on the roof was foreseeable and the school could have taken further steps to prevent this. Nevertheless the school cannot be held liable. The standard is that of reasonable care and the school are not required to take every preventative measure possible. At their age, the boys may be deemed to have consented to the risk of injury (see s.2(3)). They had to overcome obvious hurdles to gain access to the roof and they were sufficiently old to have knowledge of the risks. The act of bouncing onto a skylight was particularly reckless and not an event that the school ought to have foreseen or guarded against.

Q2. The facts in this problem are more or less identical to *McGlone v BRB*. This case should be followed. The standard of care incumbent upon the defenders is to take reasonable care and this standard has been discharged by the provision of a high fence and warning signs. The purser has had a considerable barrier to overcome and the fact that he has been able to do so does not render the defenders liable. He may be held to have consented to the risk. As a 12-year-old he would have been able to read the warning signs and would have been fully aware of the dangers.

Q3. The facts in this problem are more or less identical to those in *Titchener v BRB*. That case should be followed. Once more, the pursuers, given their ages can be held to have consented to the risk of injury.

Question

Consider the possibility of an action in either defamation or verbal injury in each of the following "newspaper articles", together with the potential for defending any such action.

1. **The Edinburgh Fringe**

The usual rubbish prevails. Return of the son of Frankenstein is particularly crass this year, with a cast of emaciated and stammering has-beens murdering Gordon Bennett's fine script. The male lead, Richard Beard could at least remember his lines, but talk about wooden! As well get Mark McManus to play King Lear. The worst acting I have seen since David Bowie in Merry Christmas Mr Lawrence, but not nearly so funny.

2. In The Courts

Senga Sneddon is appealing against the decision of the Industrial Tribunal which held that she had not been unfairly dismissed by her employers, Shank's Hosiery.

Her dismissal followed allegations that she had been stealing credit cards from customers and that she had been generally rude and abusive. Ms Sneddon had been taking cards for payment and returning store cards. She would wrap the receipt around a store card and hand it to unwary customers while slipping the customers' Access and Visa cards under the till, said Mrs Bloater, the shop manageress.

Ms Sneddon alleges she is the victim of a campaign to get rid of her. The court heard how Mrs Bloater was strict with shop floor personnel to the point that one witness, Danny Dingle, described her as a "swine to work for".

Ms Sneddon denies the allegations and told reporters outside the court "That Bloater is just out to get me...silly tart". Ms Sneddon then made various allegations on the propriety of her late employer. Staff at Shanks were unable to confirm details of liaisons said to have occurred with a Mr Grainger in menswear.

3. Out and About

Aogan Runnidgh reports from a local eatery. This week he was not impressed.

The Gung Ho Restaurant

The food, when it finally came, was diabolical. The crispy aromatic duck must have died from old age. The seaweed seemed genuine enough. It tasted like it came from Ardrossan Beach, near ICI. And I understand that it is not actually illegal to serve dog in a restaurant in this country, but it should be.

Notes for answers
Q1. The comments made are offensive to Frank Beard and he may feel that they cast a slur on his professional abilities. An accusation of professional incompetence is actionable in defamation. See, *e.g. Simmers v Morton* and *Cadzow v District Commissioners of Edinburgh.* However,

any such action could be defended on grounds of fair comment since the source of the remarks is a review in a newspaper on a matter of public interest. The public have an interest in reading informed criticism on matters such as theatre performances. Considerable latitude is allowed reviewers to provide forthright opinions "even when that opinion is couched in vituperative or contumelious language", per Lord McLaren in *Archer v Ritchie*.

In order for this defence to succeed the defender must establish three points. First that the offending passage was a comment on facts; secondly that the facts are truly stated; and thirdly the facts must concern some matter of public interest. Provided it is established that Richard Beard did in fact play the role attributed to him in the play it is difficult to see why this defence should not succeed.

Mark McManus has no action since it is a matter of trite law that one cannot defame the dead.

Q2. Senga Sneddon may well feel she has been defamed by this article. It may tend to "lower her in the estimation of right thinking people generally", per Lord Atkin in *Sim v Stretch*. The paper creates the clear impression that she is a thief although it may be arguable whether it is defamatory to suggest that a person is rude and abusive.

Mrs Bloater cannot be held liable in defamation, because the remarks she made were spoken as a witness in an industrial tribunal and as such, attract absolute privilege. A defamation action raised against her will be ruled irrelevant. Provided what is written is a fair and accurate report of the proceedings before the tribunal the newspaper's comments attract qualified privilege. That means that in order to succeed in a case against the newspaper Senga Sneddon would have to prove malice on the part of the paper.

It is not clear whether the description of Mrs Bloater as "a swine to work for" defames her or is merely abusive. On the other hand the suggestion that she waged a campaign to get rid of a member of staff is defamatory. However these accusations appear to have been made by a witness in the tribunal, accordingly they are absolutely privileged. Again, presuming the newspaper report is a fair and accurate account of the proceedings, their comments attract qualified privilege. To sue the paper successfully on this ground, Mrs Bloater would have to prove malice.

Mrs Bloater may well have a case against Senga Sneddon in respect of the words spoken outside court. The expression "silly tart" is probably just abuse and not actionable; would readers think that this was a serious imputation that Mrs Bloater carried on the business of a prostitute? Possibly the defence of "in rixa" might apply (see, *e.g. Christie v Robertson*) for words spoken in the heat of the moment. This defence might also apply to Senga Sneddon's suggestion that Mrs Bloater is vindictive. This statement could be defamatory and of course words spoken out of court are not protected by privilege. The newspaper is on shaky ground in reporting this outburst and may be liable in defamation unless they can show this as a matter of public interest attracting qualified privilege.

Finally the newspaper should never have printed the allegation of liaisons with Mr Grainger. While not *prima facie* defamatory since "liaisons" could involve business matters it is likely that the reader would impute sexual connotations to the allegation. In circumstances of employment it might be defamatory to suggest that Mrs Bloater, a married woman (though we do not know if Mr Bloater is still in the picture) has been "carrying on" with a colleague. Mrs Bloater would have to establish innuendo. Do the words bear a defamatory meaning? What would readers have assumed the words to mean? If Mrs Bloater can establish a defamatory meaning then both Senga Sneddon and the paper may be liable to her in damages. Senga Sneddon may offer to prove the truth of the allegations by running the defence of "veritas". If she succeeds this is a complete defence. The paper will try to seek qualified privilege on grounds that they have reported a matter of public interest, but this must be doubtful. The paper seems merely to have repeated an item of malicious gossip.

Q3. The Gung Ho restaurant cannot be defamed. This may be a case of verbal injury rather than defamation. This is an example of what may be termed "slander of business". The pursuers will have to establish the meaning that readers would take from the comments, particularly the final line which suggests, though it does not actually say so, that the restaurant serves dog.

The paper and author would run the defence of fair comment (see answer to Q1 for details). It may be however, that these remarks go beyond comment on the facts and the facts may not be truly stated, unless that is, dog really was served. This seems unlikely. It will be for the restaurant to prove malice and also to prove the falsity of the statements. This will not be easy to prove, but there may be some "history" between the parties. Certainly, the review does seem malicious.

INDEX